THE PREPPER'S SURVIVAL BIBLE

Learn Nuclear and Biological War Survival Skills, Stockpiling, Canning, Emergency Medicine. Life-Saving Strategies to Survive Anywhere.

John White

Copyright © 2022 - All rights reserved John White

The content contained within this book may not be reproduced, duplicated, or transmitted without direct written permission from the author or the publisher.

Under no circumstances will any blame or legal responsibility be held against the publisher, or author, for any damages, reparation, or monetary loss due to the information contained within this book. Either directly or indirectly.

Legal Notice:

This book is copyright protected. This book is only for personal use. You cannot amend, distribute, sell, use, quote, or paraphrase any part, or the content within this book, without the consent of the author or publisher.

Disclaimer Notice:

Please note the information contained within this document is for educational and entertainment purposes only. All effort has been executed to present accurate, up-to-date, and reliable, complete information. No warranties of any kind are declared or implied. Readers acknowledge that the author is not engaging in the rendering of legal, financial, medical, or professional advice. The content within this book has been derived from various sources. Please consult a licensed professional before attempting any techniques outlined in this book.

By reading this document, the reader agrees that under no circumstances is the author responsible for any losses, direct or indirect, which are incurred as a result of the use of the information contained within this document, including, but not limited to, — errors, omissions, or inaccuracies.

Table of Contents

Introduction

A disaster happens when a situation rapidly gets worse due to uncontrollable circumstances. It is best to have an emergency plan with the essentials of what to do in these situations when going about your daily life.

What Constitutes the Essentials?

They are actions that must be taken either before or after a major disaster. For instance, a strong earthquake will cause damage, casualties, and numerous other disasters. In essence, an emergency plan is created before these disasters strike. You will need to know what to do when it is time for them.

Disasters can strike both at home and when you're away. However, a prepper is someone who has made preparations for disasters that aren't always predicted. Preppers need to know what they can do before a disaster occur and what to do when it does.

Fundamentally speaking, Prepping is just shorthand for the phrases "preparation" or "preparing," but its usage in recent times has expanded significantly. The term is now used to describe prepping for disaster situations and significant tragedies. Although it covers such fundamentals as storing food, water, medications, and other essentials, it extends far more than that.

Ultimately, we want to be ready for potential disasters and have the means of surviving them. If you're already outside when a disaster strikes, you'll also want to find refuge for your family. Make sure you have a plan in place in case something unexpected happens.

Be mindful of nature

Nature needs to be protected; thus, you must leave it alone. This implies that you cannot dig up your well, fill in your pond, or paint over rainwater tanks. You risk running out of water if you do that.

The power grid is down, and you need to protect it

Your area won't always be as secure as it was before a crisis or disaster that led to a power loss. Usually, when the lights go off, there is looting. It could be weeks or months before your electricity returns.

Defend your home from burglars

Looters are one of the greatest threats during a crisis. They are searching for the simple victim and will try to steal whatever they can from unprotected residences, businesses, automobiles, and trucks.

Staying Healthy in a Disaster

Getting food and water might be difficult when the power goes out. Make sure you have a stock of canned food and bottled water. If you prefer the atmosphere of campfires, an electric campfire stove is an alternative and a camping stove.

Since many individuals are unaware of how simple it is to catch infections from contaminated water, clean water is also crucial. You can either boil the water or buy a cheap solar shower.

Keeping Your Family Safe

It would help if you were ready for the potential that not everyone in your family will be there when a disaster strikes. It's crucial to have strategies in place for bringing the family back together if this occurs.

Get a communication technique as your first step. To call them if they aren't home when you are, you can achieve this by obtaining a HAM radio license or by providing each member of the household with a charged cell phone.

Examine evacuation strategies

Your evacuation plan will differ based on where you live, but most people believe they can leave a disaster-stricken area quickly by driving away from the scene.

You should be aware of traffic closures, damaged bridges or tunnels, and other conditions affecting evacuation routes.

But what will you do if you are unable to drive?

Being financially prepared

Being financially prepared can help you endure unforeseen disasters. You can manage financial challenges during a crisis by having an emergency fund for disaster scenarios. People frequently put off dealing with their finances once they have more time.

Go Green

Being green entails caring for Mother Earth in general and being ready for disasters. For instance, considering that a generator operates on gas, you would believe that gasoline is the most significant choice.

However, generators are only sometimes dependable enough to run continuously for 20 hours. An alternative would be to purchase a 3-kilowatt generator that runs on gas or butane.

Try to think outside the box

We all consider what we would do in the event of a disaster, but how prepared are you? Consider unconventional ideas and give them a go. During a crisis, you can learn some amazing things and enjoy things you otherwise wouldn't even be aware of.

Even though none of these disasters may impact your town, you and your family may still experience some of them. Make sure you're prepared for any disaster by following these tips. Be ready to survive!

CHAPTER 1
Prepping Basics

You can get yourself, your home, and your family ready by thinking about your specific situation and the kinds of emergencies that are most likely to happen in it. Being prepared can mean different things to different people, like ensuring your home is safe from burglars or your pantry and first aid kit are well-stocked.

But in every case, figuring out where to start is the most important and often most challenging step.

Different eventualities are covered by prepper preparation. Because they have a forward- thinking perspective, they can adapt to any emergency.

The many types of scenarios that preppers prepare for will be covered in this chapter.

1. Different types of scenarios that preppers prepare for.
2. How to start Preparing.
3. Fundamental Concepts.
4. Shtf Survival Plan

How to Start Prepping?

Natural disasters can be challenging to foresee, but happily, there are techniques to reduce your risk of experiencing one. Apply these tips on disaster prevention to be ready for anything! These disaster prevention suggestions will ensure you're prepared in the case of a disaster, from creating an emergency kit to ensuring you understand how your property is covered.

It is crucial to be ready in case of a disaster in your neighborhood. Disasters can happen at any time and are unpredictable. However, being organized can help you avert or lessen the effects of a disaster.

- Find out if an alternative evacuation route doesn't go through trees or over hills during severe storms from where you live, work, or study.
- Plan for comfort and safety if there is no electricity.
- Create a family evacuation plan for emergencies.
- Know where your neighbors reside, work, or attend school so you can assist them if necessary.
- Please fill up your petrol tank before a significant storm to avoid having a severe fuel shortage after it passes.
- Learn what to do if there is a threat of an active shooter if you work in or near a school.
- If you're providing emergency services at your home, place of business, or place of worship, check for gas leaks before a storm or while you shower. This will stop houses and businesses from being destroyed by fire.
- Avoid overloading extension cables and appliances with bulky items like furniture and clothing; doing so could result in fire if the cords get tangled in a wall heater, portable heater, or other appliance nearby.
- Place all fire-starting items, including fireplaces and logs, flower pots, stoves, grills, outdoor heaters, and other appliances, at least six feet above the ground.
- Distance yourself more from tall buildings. If it is safe, stay inside your high-rise building if you live there. Take the stairs unless there is another item that will stop you from falling, like a railing.

- Ensure your home is equipped with fire extinguishers, particularly those used inside.
- Always keep an emergency kit packed and ready to use. A battery-operated or hand- crank radio, extra lanterns and batteries, a first aid kit, food, water, and different medication should all be included in your gear.

Fundamental Concept of Prepping

It's crucial to pack the right backpack with everything you'll need to live before you choose a camp and begin exploring the woods, but roughing it doesn't mean you have to plan. In this chapter, we will help you identify the necessary equipment, tools, and clothing items for living outside.

1. *Survivalist's Tool Kit: Essentials for preparing for any eventuality.*

It is crucial to plan for as many potential situations as possible in the wilderness because they are numerous. You can navigate with a compass, although a handheld GPS gadget is preferable. In the dark, flashlights and glow sticks can help you navigate, and a flare gun can help people find you in an emergency.

A tarp, cable ties, duct tape, and paracord are necessary for camp. Gloves, a folding shovel, and a decent multi-tool are also essential. Include water-resistant matches, a lighter, and a fire starter kit; redundancy is a good thing in this case. Fishhooks and lines, razor blades, sewing needles and thread, safety pins, nails, a small magnet, and some money should all be kept in a small tin.

2. *Packing Tips: A few easy suggestions for your backpack.*

Your comfort and safety are thought to require a well-packed backpack. Muscle discomfort and unnecessary pressure on your backbone result from poor weight distribution. Water, food, and cooking tools should be placed in the center of your pack, near your body. Use medium-weight materials like clothing, tarps, and rain gear to secure the heavier objects and cushion them, so they do not shift while you are hiking.

Your sleeping bag should be kept in your backpack's back pocket or tied to the bottom. Put things like a compass, a map, sunglasses, toilet paper, a trowel, sunscreen, insect repellent, a pocketknife, a flashlight, food, and a small towel in the side and exterior compartments of your backpack.

3. Clothing: Dress with layers.

Temperatures might change significantly over a day depending on the geographic area of the wilderness region you are traveling in and the time of year. To conserve heat and keep yourself light, layer your clothing.

A fleece jacket, windbreaker, and waterproof outer jacket should be adequate for worst- case scenarios. Gloves, a hat, and a headband complete your outfit, along with a pair of sandals and water shoes.

4. Practical multi-tools: Essential survival gear.

A great multi-tool is a camper's best buddy for versatility, and numerous varieties are available. Less complicated is preferable when weighing the desire for the best capabilities against the weight of the equipment. Look for a multi-tool with a bottle and can opener, pliers with a twine cutter, a carbide knife sharpener, an ordinary and serrated blade, and a lanyard loop.

Look for titanium handles, 154CM metallic blades, and 420 stainless steel construction; pay particular attention to the materials and quality. Consider a multi-tool hatchet as an alternative if you plan to carry a small hatchet for cutting firewood.

5. Food: Items to bring.

Whether you're traveling by car or walking far into the woods, the kind and quantity of food you bring will differ.

Most camping supply stores carry a range of pre-packaged meals, or you can prepare them yourself.

Plan a menu of quick, light, and simple dishes. Consider taking dehydrated items you can prepare with hot water if you are hauling everything in your bag.

6. *Ready-to-eat meals: add water.*

Pre-packaged meals are the ideal camping food because they are portable, practical, and straightforward.

There are a lot of prepared meals available for purchase; you may buy them in bulk, select the food variety you like, and enjoy preparing your own.

Try having 1/3 cup of dry couscous for lunch and 1/2 cup of freeze-dried vegetables.

7. *Cloths and Bandanas.*

Bandanas can be used for various purposes, take up very little space, and even be worn as jewelry. Use it as a tourniquet, wound dressing, smoke mask, or sling as medical equipment.

Make a sweatband, tie your hair back, or cover your head with a hat to protect it from the sun. A bandana in a vivid color gives a visible signal if you become lost or disoriented; cut strips to mark your trail.

Shtf Plan Survival

Use these SHTF plan survival tips to be ready for the worst!

Natural disasters can be challenging to foresee, but happily, there are techniques to reduce your risk of experiencing one.

These SHTF plan survival advice can ensure you're prepared in the case of a disaster, from creating an emergency bag to ensuring you understand how your home is insured.

It's crucial to be ready in case of a disaster in your neighborhood.

Disasters can happen at any time and are unpredictable.

However, being organized can help you avert or lessen the effects of a disaster.

The various categories of fundamental concept scenarios will be covered in this section.

Survival scenarios for wildlife

Preppers become ready for wild wildlife survival scenarios. Examples of such systems include being shipwrecked on an uninhabited island or getting lost while hiking and ending up stranded in the woods.

Self-Defense scenarios

People who support the prepper movement are also prepared to deal with violent encounters of any kind. They are aware of their legal repercussions and know how to defend themselves.

Examples of these scenarios include being robbed or getting into a fight.

Long-lasting and transient natural disasters

Preppers prepare for potential natural disasters like tornadoes, floods, earthquakes, or wildfires bound to strike their region.

They construct specialized shelters and stockpile many goods, including food, water, and medical supplies, to be ready for such scenarios.

Warfare Using Bio chemicals

Another eventuality that preppers plan for is biochemical warfare. They prepare disposable coveralls, boots, gloves, and face respirators since they are worried about avoiding lethal illnesses.

Influences of Population Decline

Worldwide human population growth may impact the supply of food, fresh water, oil, and other basic human needs.

Preppers, therefore, strive to be self-sufficient even if society collapses.

Financial Crisis

Past monetary disasters include the Great Depression and the Lehman Shock. Despite this, preppers are constantly prepared in the event of a financial collapse. They hold precious metal reserves and invest in mining shares because they think the Federal Reserve System is defective.

They anticipate that paper money will lose all of its value during hyperinflation.

Scriptural Rapture

While not all preppers are religious, some make plans in case the rapture described in the Bible occurs.

However, religious extremists also prepare for such a situation by building food reserves and other supplies.

The Mind of Survival

Making a fire or building a shelter is not the first task in outdoor survival. It would be best if you first cultivated the mindset of a true survivor before doing any of the things.

Find a real-life survival tale, and you'll discover that the people who made it through had similar mental traits that helped them cope with their challenging circumstances.

Developing a survivor's mindset is incredibly important, and the top five qualities you'll need are listed below:

1. A positive outlook

It's not necessary to view having a positive outlook as another cliché just because practically all survival books stress its relevance.

A positive attitude is necessary. It is also one of the most complex skills to learn, but the effort will be worthwhile.

If you consistently adopt this mindset, you will be prepared if you ever find yourself lost in the wilderness.

2. *Motivation*

What is the single thing that can inspire someone to continue living even when everything else around them is failing? Many tales of survival touch on the survivor's adherence to non- secular ideas or a higher power as a source of inspiration and hope.

Other survivors have also talked about how crucial it was for them to return to their friends, family, and loved ones. What do you think will motivate you to survive in a survival situation? It would be best if you made that choice because it is different for each person.

3. *Mental toughness*

This does not refer to physical prowess, endurance, pain tolerance, or the number of calluses you possess. Your determination and mental perseverance together make up your mental strength.

To become mentally strong, you must endure the intolerable, put up with the immoral, overcome your decision to give up, and overcome all your flaws.

4. *Adaptation*

Survival and adaptability are intertwined. Think about how animals and plants survive.

Those who couldn't change with the environment didn't make it. Those who changed and developed survived.

You must adjust to all the shifting circumstances, settings, and occurrences. You should know what should be abandoned and what should be kept.

5.   *Work Ethic*

Another essential component of your survival attitude is your work ethic. Being in a challenging situation frequently inspires people to work harder and improve their future, provided that one exists.

A person with a strong work ethic and someone who never gives up is a true survivor. Your strong work ethic could make up for the things you weren't fortunate enough to have.

CHAPTER 2
Canned Food

You will discover a description of correct canning techniques and information about how canning works and why it is safe and cost-effective.

Whether you've canned food at home or this is your first time, it's essential to read and follow the directions carefully. While experimenting with different amounts or additional ingredients, it's vital to follow others precisely as specified.

Many recipes say whether or not you should use your imagination, but if you need more time, err on the side of caution. You might have too-runny jam, mushy vegetables, or damaged goods if you don't.

If you take the time to follow the instructions and adequately prepare your food and equipment, you will find that home canning is secure, affordable, incredibly fulfilling, and a lot of fun.

Food preparedness (Best Survival Foods to Stockpile)

What are the best meals for a survival situation at this level to stockpile? What do you want to acquire right away, while you still have access to money, before it's too late and anarchy breaks out?

What are the best emergency foods for survival?

Catastrophic disasters can take many different forms. Recent years have demonstrated that a catastrophic disaster can occur anytime and anywhere. A terrorist assault using a WMD or the dreaded EMP attack, which cuts off power in a nation for weeks and disrupts shipping and transportation, might cause a severe food shortage.

Start getting ready by storing the best survival supplies, so you are ready for anything, whether a man-made disaster or an unanticipated natural disaster.

You'll want items that help you satisfy nutritional goals, have high-calorie content, and are simple meals that are likely to disappear first from pantries, whether in a pinch or planning many weeks.

The optimal food for survival strikes a balance between weight and caloric and nutritional content. If you also plan to bring survival gear, you must pay special attention to this.

If need be, it will be difficult to move with a significant amount of canned food because it is heavy and immobile. However, you must include canned food in your survival diet since, if you don't have to escape or travel, it can be the only thing that helps you get through the first several weeks (especially on foot).

You should always carry a survival multi-tool when you have canned food (instead of a can opener). One-use tools, like can openers, should generally be avoided.

The Best Foods for Survival

1. Canned wild Alaskan salmon

Salmon from Alaska that has been canned is high in protein and healthy fats like omega 3. You can discover salmon with little to no environmental toxins by searching for "Alaskan wild salmon," which can occasionally be found in other canned fish from other regions of the world. Salmon may not be your favorite food, but you should know that Inuit people, who live in Alaska and northern Canada, are known for having low heart attacks and stroke rates on a traditional diet. This is because they consume fish continuously for a long period.

Like canned tuna, Alaskan wild salmon can be consumed straight from the can without having to prepare it.

Plan to share the salmon with two to three other people at a time if refrigeration is not a possibility so nothing goes to waste. It is at the top of our list of the greatest survival meals due to its long shelf life and exceptional protein content. It also has great flavor!

2. Brown rice

Along with important vitamins and minerals like iron, brown rice is a good source of calories and protein. Brown rice has a long shelf life and is a dry, non-perishable meal, making it an excellent survival food. However, brown rice has one drawback: typically, it must be boiled for a number of minutes.

Sometimes, whether or not that's on a propane, butane, or wood-burning stove, the last thing you need to do in a long-term situation where there isn't electricity accessible is spend precious fuel cooking food for this amount of time.

Therefore, "brown rice warm cereal" is probably preferable for a prolonged survival emergency where you are stocking up your pantry because it cooks in just five to eight minutes while remaining packed with nutrients and calories (one cup of brown rice warm cereal contains 600 calories, 12 grams of protein, and 16% of the daily recommended amount of iron and is easily rationed out into smaller quantities).

3. Dried legumes

A meal of kidney beans, black beans, garbanzo beans, lima beans, pinto beans, and other beans has a lot of protein, several critical vitamins, and minerals. Compared to canned beans, dried beans are more readily available and weigh less.

The main distinction is that before eating most beans, you must add water and let them soak for many hours. For instance, split peas need less time to soak. Split peas share some of the same vitamins and minerals as the dried bean family.

In the end, dried beans have long shelf lives. Dried beans can be stored for a long time in the car trunk, the survival kit in the office, and the survival pantry at your home or lodge.

4. *Large nuts*

Look for unsalted and unshelled nuts in the bulk seed and nut area of your local supermarket (if possible). You should select ingredients for survival that include little salt. The bulk food department of grocery stores often sells a variety of nuts and seeds that are high in vital vitamins, minerals, essential fatty acids, and protein.

These include peanuts, almonds, sunflower seeds, and other nuts and seeds. Furthermore, they are fairly lightweight. Spend money on airtight food storage containers, such as glass jars or plastic packing containers, at the same time.

Although most bulk dry foods may last up to a few months (check expiration dates), if maintained in a nice, dark environment, you can extend shelf life by putting those in the refrigerator.

5. *Peanut butter*

It also contains variety of vital nutrients and minerals, is rich in protein and necessary fatty acids, and (including copper and iron). Select "natural" brands like Skippy Natural Peanut Butter for the healthiest alternative.

During a disaster, one of your methods to survive is to realize that it's time to decrease calories - most individuals consume more calories per day than they need to survive. Just a couple of tablespoons of peanut butter a day can help a person continue to survive.

By reducing calories, you can extend the shelf life of your food while also losing weight (which will make getting out on foot sooner or later simpler than if you are dragging around additional weight).

6. *A trail mix*

The trail mix is a favorite among hikers and contains a range of ingredients, including raisins, peanuts, various nuts and frequent chocolate pieces.

The simple carbohydrates found in raisins, chocolate, and dried fruit may act as a temporary mood enhancer and source of energy. Dried fruit can be a part of your survival diet by using trail mix.

7. *Bars of chocolate and energy*

There are energy bars in every taste imaginable. In addition to having a lot of protein and a variety of nutrients, look for brands with a high-calorie count. Chocolate bars are high in calories and can be a quick source of energy as well as a great mood booster.

In the days and weeks that follow a disaster, chocolate is likely to become a commodity in high demand.

8. *Beef jerky*

For beef, turkey, and other meat, look for "natural" products that don't have as many or any of the bad components as other jerky brands. A delectable kind of dried beef is jerky. Native Americans, American pioneers, and other agrarian societies all around the world have long used dried beef as a survival food.

While traditional methods of making "jerky" used methods like smoking and sun drying, modern industrial methods of drying meat accomplish this on a far larger scale. Your choices are: You have two options: buy your dried meat in bulk and have it shipped to you personally, or purchase the smaller serving packages at the supermarket.

9. *Espresso or instant coffee*

Even if you don't, someone in your company probably does and may feel drained, lethargic, and get headaches without coffee (or caffeine).

Coffee does not have to be a major priority, but having access to it will undoubtedly make many people in your group happy.

It boosts morale and improves mood temporarily. And it is still another thing that might be traded in a crisis, like a commodity.

10. Sea vegetables and super veggies in powder

These days, sea veggies that may be purchased as tablets or powder are a common product sold in health food stores. Most localities will be low on fresh produce during a disaster. Sea veggies are excellent meals since they are packed with vitamins, nutrients, and health benefits that boost immunity, promote tissue repair, and speed wound healing.

They might have anti-bacterial and anti-fungal qualities. They can be powdered after being dried; therefore the name "powdered super veggies." This implies that sea veggies like kelp and chlorella make for delicious meals.

Even though I put sea vegetables at number 10, they really ought to be the top survival food on this list of the top ten. Again, the point is that during a severe emergency, fresh vegetables may become scarce or disappear entirely in some areas.

Canning (Why Can Foods?)

A fun and smart technique to protect your priceless product is canning. City dwellers are learning how gratifying it is to make seasonal goodies linger all year round as more farmers' markets are expanding into metropolitan areas.

Canning your own or locally grown food may save you 50% off the price of purchasing commercially canned food in addition to the worth of your effort. What could be nicer or more considerate than a jar of handmade jam that has been specially crafted to include the recipient's preferred fruits and flavors?

A bonus of home canning is the nutritional benefits. As soon as veggies are harvested, many of them start to lose their vitamins. If the fresh produce is not kept cool or stored, nearly half the vitamins may be lost in a few days.

Even refrigerated produce loses half or more of several vitamins in just one to two weeks.

Between one-third and fifty percent of the vitamins A and C, thiamin, and riboflavin are destroyed during the heating process of canning.

Foods that have been canned may lose between 5% and 20% of these delicate vitamins annually.

But when compared to fresh food, the amounts of other vitamins in canned food are just somewhat reduced. If vegetables are handled carefully and put in jars as soon as possible after being picked, they can have more nutrients than fresh food sold in nearby stores.

When you start with low-quality goods, when jars don't seal properly, when food spoils, and when flavors, textures, colors, and nutrients degrade over time in storage, the benefits of home canning are lost.

The following advice outlines many of these issues and suggests solutions.

How Canning Preserves Foods?

The majority of fresh foods are extremely perishable due to their high water content. For a variety of causes, they degrade or lose their quality.

- Growth of bacteria, molds, and yeasts, which are unfavorable microorganisms
- Enzyme activity in food
- Reactions to oxygen
- Microorganisms thrive and swiftly multiply on the exteriors of fresh food as well as on the interiors of food that has been rotten, bitten by an insect. Fresh food tissues contain both oxygen and enzymes.

Suitable canning procedures include:

- Selecting and cleaning fresh food with care
- Peeling a few new foods
- Hot packing a lot of food
- Some dishes can be prepared by adding acids (lemon juice, citric acid, or vinegar).
- Utilizing suitable containers and self-sealing lids

Processing jars in boiling water or pressure canner for the right length of time results in the removal of oxygen, the destruction of enzymes, the prevention of unwanted bacteria, yeast, and mold growth, and the formation of a high vacuum inside the jars.

High vacuums create tight seals that retain liquid within while keeping air and microbes outside.

Proper Canning Techniques

Developing Clostridium botulin bacteria in canned food can result in botulism, a potentially fatal food illness. These bacteria can be found as vegetative cells or as spores.

The spores, which resemble plant seeds, may endure in soil and water for a very long time without harm. The spores generate vegetative cells when growth conditions are favorable; these cells multiply quickly and could create a lethal toxin in three to four days in the following conditions:

- An acid-free, moist food
- A temperature of 40 to 120 degrees Fahrenheit, and
- Less than 2% oxygen is present.

The majority of fresh food surfaces contain botulinum spores. They are safe to eat on fresh meals because they can only grow in the absence of air. The majority of bacteria, yeasts, and molds are challenging to get off food surfaces.

Washing fresh food only marginally lowers their population. Peeling tomatoes, underground stem crops, and root crops significantly lower their populations. Blanching is beneficial, but canning techniques and following advised processing periods based on research are the most important controls.

These processing intervals guarantee that the majority of heat-resistant microbes in home- canned goods are destroyed.

If lids are sealed, and jars are kept below 95°F, properly sterilized canned food won't go bad. Jars retain quality better when kept at a temperature of 50 to 70°F.

Dehydrated Foods

Fruits and Vegetables

Fruits and vegetables that have been dehydrated are a terrific addition to the emergency food supply. They really retain more nutrients thanks to the processing method than either their canned or frozen equivalents.

Most dry foods with only one ingredient are prepared without salt, which is a huge bonus for my family.

Compared to canned green beans, which have 380 mg of salt per serving, dried green beans have 0 mg.

You can freeze-dry or dry fruits and vegetables. Jerky, raisins, fruit roll-ups, potato flakes, and seasoning soup mix are just a few examples of the dried foods we see in the grocery store. Dried foods are a typical component of many people's diets.

You can dry your chosen food at home by using low heat. Up to 98 percent of the food's moisture can be removed during drying, leaving you with little, and lighter storage.

Dried goods can be kept in your cupboard for one to three years if they are properly stored.

A more advanced technique for drying food is called freeze-drying, which enables the food to keep its nutrients as well as its flavor, color, and shape.

A #10 can of freeze-dried veggies offers forty to fifty servings and weighs less than three pounds, making it even lighter than dried meals.

In general, freeze-dried foods have a far longer shelf life than traditional dry goods—up to 25 years for an unopened container.

I always have dehydrated vegetables on hand to use as soup or stew bases or as flavorings in my cooking. Our pantry also has some pre-made soup blends, dried onion flakes, Chile and bell peppers, carrots, celery, mushrooms, spinach, broccoli, and garlic. For producing potato soup and mashed potatoes, we also retain potato flakes.

Healthy snacks like dried fruits are excellent. You can keep dried apples, apricots, bananas, dates, prunes, and raisins in your pantry's section designated for snacks. Fruit that has been reconstituted can be used in the same way as canned or frozen fruit.

Planning Your Long-Term Storage Pantry

Consider your plan for long-term food storage as a "food bank account." You want that bank account to be a wise investment, one that you can easily access, and one that will give you the exact funds you require at the precise moment you require them.

Remember: Storing food you don't want to consume serves no use, regardless of how cheap it is, how long it will last, or how useful it may seem.

What therefore should you store in your pantry?

Store What You Eat and Eat What You Store

Using the sensible maxim "consumes what you store, store what you eat," create your own customized food pantry. In other words, you don't stockpile food and put it up for some

imagined future time; instead, you only buy food you truly want to eat, food your family is used to eating, and food you actually use every day. You don't need to wait for a serious emergency to use your food because you regularly go through your pantry.

Even if your budget is a little tight for just a week, you always have your own piggy bank to pull from. Think about the kind of meals your family already consumes before you begin building your own personalized food store. Examine your favorite recipes to see if you can modify them to include ingredients from the pantry. When planning and storing meals, always try to be as balanced as possible.

CHAPTER 3
Weather Preparedness

Water Supply

You must learn to meet your fundamental needs, such as food, water, and shelter if you want to survive in the wild. Additionally, you must learn how to build a fire, navigate the terrain, and treat wounds. Learn the fundamentals of each of these abilities in turn in this chapter.

Finding and maintaining a water supply should always be your top priority while trying to survive in the wild.

Even while your body can go for weeks without food for sustenance, after just a few days without water, you risk dying of dehydration.

Furthermore, long before dehydration becomes fatal, you may become paralyzed and noticeably lose cognitive function, which will hinder you from optimizing your chances of survival.

Ultimately, you must understand that finding water takes precedence over immediate survival issues in most outdoor survival situations. If you are stranded in the bush and must survive for an extended period of time, keep searching for water and don't stop looking.

Advice on where to obtain water is tough to give because it relies so much on the geology of the area and the type of biome you are thinking about in your survival scenario.

Although it is completely outside the scope of this book to explore and provide knowledge for every environmental possibility, there are some general water-locating tactics and patterns that you might be able to use if you find yourself in a tight spot.

However, there are a few opening remarks to be made beforehand.

It is always preferable to make an effort to filter or purify water before drinking it, no matter where you get it from. Boiling water is a great approach to getting rid of the majority of germs and other hazardous organisms that your water may be concealing if you have the time and resources.

More practically, when time and money are scarce, you might not be able to boil your water, but you should at least try to filter it to get rid of dirt, insects, and any parasites.

For the goal of filtering water, several man-made survival items are available, but simpler techniques include passing water through fabric or a dense mass of leaves or bark, which can also be effective.

Similar to this, always choose moving freshwater such as rivers and gullies over still bodies of water like lakes and ponds. Moving water makes it less likely for biological hazards like bacteria that can cause illness to exist there.

Now that this has been established, you can appreciate how to find water. The plants and animals in your immediate area can be your biggest potential allies when you're trying to find water. There probably is a noteworthy supply of water nearby if a place is highly vegetated and lush. Birds and bug swarms will also gather around water sources.

Keep an eye on the nearby fauna; wherever it congregates, water is likely to be present.

Also, keep in mind that gravity dictates that water will always flow downward. Find your sources of water by scanning the horizon for low-lying areas. In many places, including those where the ground appears to be frequently wet or saturated, water can also be found below the surface.

If you can, try to dig a hole a few feet down and wait a few minutes; you can see that water starts to naturally pool there. As a word of warning, if you do locate water in this manner, put extra effort into carefully filtering it.

Water can also be obtained by catching it in the dew, rain, snow, or ice, among other sources. When it rains, spread out whatever containers you have to collect water, making careful to maximize the available surface area. If you have a waterproof material, you can use it to temporarily cover a ditch or tiny hole in order to collect water.

Of course, water can also be produced by melting ice or snow.

However, keep in mind that if the weather is cold enough to support ice or snow, you should always be sure you melt it first. A decreased body temperature might also cause water to evaporate via the skin.

Finally, utilizing cloth to absorb water from adjacent plants and then straining that fabric will allow you to gather water from dew. Naturally, early in the morning is the optimum time to gather dew because it has not yet been evaporated by the rising light and is still airborne water that has collected on the nearby vegetation.

Water Storage

The most important component for survival is water. Despite the discomfort that hunger can bring, the majority of us are capable of going days or even weeks without eating. But we cannot survive without water for a week.

Actually, the average person could probably only survive three to five days without water in a reasonably pleasant setting while exerting very little energy.

Even something as simple as an energy outage might completely disrupt your daily schedule. Your pump will suddenly stop functioning, putting that tap water just out of reach. Because of this, you should always have enough potable water on hand to last everyone and every pet in the house for at least three days.

That amounts to around a gallon each day for adults and large canines. Smaller animals and children might be able to survive with less. This means that you should always have at least 12 gallons of drinking water in bottles on hand for a family of four. An additional gallon per person would also be ideal for cleaning and hygiene.

Wells and municipal water systems may be damaged or contaminated by floods and storms, thus making it impossible to access resources for prolonged periods of time. It's difficult to maintain a three-month supply of water since it is so heavy. That is 90 gallons only for drinking, each person. For hygienic and personal purposes, budget an additional gallon each day. Filling your own food-grade containers with tap water is a smart place to start because it is safe to store.

Consider using water storage barrels for big amounts of water. Each barrel holds up to 55 gallons or approximately a month's worth for two people. Food-grade 55 gallon drums are relatively simple to fill and store, although they weigh more than 400 pounds when completely filled.

Smaller containers, particularly 5-gallon drums, are what we prefer to store. Every size of packaged water is available, from single-serve bottles to sealed 5 gallon containers, and many of them can be used again as water storage.

Maintain water in a cool, dark location. It won't harm it if it freezes, but it might cause overfilled containers to leak. Although there is no set expiration date for water, it doesn't harm to check large containers for cloudiness before using. Long-lasting freshness is expected from sealed containers.

Consider storing water containers there as well if your freezer isn't already packed. As the frozen water containers melt, they will serve as an additional source of water and assist keep the freezer cool for longer. Just be careful to leave space in the containers you keep there for expansion.

Wilderness Water Purification Techniques

One of the most popular types of water filters used to cleanse water in a wilderness survival situation is the straw-type filter. The Life Straw is one of many such products available on the market. These filters function by obstructing particles larger than 0.2 microns. That's a really strong safety margin considering that the majority of germs are larger than 2 microns. One thousand liters of water can be filtered with the Life Straw.

When using a straw-style filter, place one end in the lake or stream and drink through it. Although it's really useful, you can't use it to purify water to carry in a canteen or water bottle. When researching straw-type filters, it's crucial to consider the filtering size (the 0.2 microns mentioned above) and the number of gallons the filter is capable of handling. Some straws don't filter as thoroughly or as much water as the Life Straw.

Use bag-type water filters to sanitize the water in the wasteland

A bag-style filter is something that many people also have in their bug-out bag. The main benefit of a bag-type filter over a straw-type filter is that you can pour the water through the bag- type filter and then transfer it to a canteen or water bottle for later use. This is significant because it enables you to travel farther away from the sea.

Despite not really using a bag, Life Straw also produces a filter that looks like a bag. The bag in this instance is a hard plastic cup, but the concept is the same. It provides you with an equivalent level of safety because it uses the same filter out as the other Life Straw.

The Sawyer Mini Water Filtration System, which has hollow fiber architecture, is another excellent filter. Although their design only filters down to 0.1 microns, it may last longer due to the filter's 100,000 gallon capacity.

Using pills to purify water

It's not very convenient to carry around iodine. People instead take iodine pills, such as those made by Potable Aqua. These are simple to use and provide a practical way to sanitize water in the wild. The major issue with relying on these kinds of tablets is that you ultimately run out and are left without a means of purifying water.

To utilize the pills, add water to a canteen or water bottle before inserting the tablets. Although you should include these in your survival kit, they are only effective for short-term water purification. Similar results might be obtained with regular home bleach.

The ingredient in bleach, chlorine, is also used to prevent disease growth in swimming pools and in municipal water towers. Finding a container to carry the bleach in is the answer to preventing bleach leakage over your meals and other supplies.

You will also require an eye dropper because each gallon of water requires eight drops of bleach to be purified.

Give the bleach a half-hour to kill any bacteria, just like the iodine tablets did.

Purify water in the wilderness through boiling

Boiling the water will also destroy any pathogens present. This necessitates the use of a container that won't melt or burn in a fireplace, such a canteen cup. In a pinch, you could boil water in a cup made of birch bark.

The cup won't burn as long as the flames are kept away from its base.

Purify water using solar energy in the wild

Solar-powered water purification can be accomplished by using a WAPI, or water pasteurization indicator. Submerge the WAPI in the liquid. Place the bottle where it will be exposed to direct sunlight, preferably on a surface that is black or very dark in color.

The water in the bottle will be sufficiently heated by the sun to reach the pasteurization temperature. The wax pellet in the WAPI will soften when the temperature is appropriate.

However, you should be cautious when drinking the water and make sure that only the portion of the bottle's exterior that the bottle cap covers come into contact with your lips.

Yes, excessive hydration may have negative effects, but your body needs a certain amount of water to support normal organ function. The issue is that not always can you bring potable water with you (or you can run out).

1. Boiling

Boiling water is the simplest technique to purify water, assuming you have the equipment and a campfire or camp range. Put water in a pot and heat it on high until bubbles begin to roll; let them roll for at least five minutes. After that, wait until it cools before drinking to avoid burning your lips and tongue.

2. Pumps for filtration or purification

If you go to a store that sells camping and outdoor gear, you will undoubtedly find a variety of great pumps with filters and purifiers to ensure that only drinkable water exits the

pump and goes directly into your water bottle. This is accomplished by forcing water through a ceramic or charcoal filter and chemically treating it.

This system is integrated into some high-tech water bottles, eliminating the need for you to pump water into a separate container. Instead, the purification process happens as you squeeze or suck water directly into your mouth.

3.   *Drugs and purification drops*

Using purification drops is an easy, affordable, but perhaps not the finest tasting, method of water filtration. Iodine is the most frequently utilized chemical, however potassium permanganate or chlorine are also useful.

Drink the water after it has been exposed to the chemicals for at least 20 minutes, and blend it with powdered mixes to hide any flavors.

4.   *Draw water from the earth*

All of the aforementioned tactics call for you to carry water or have access to a water supply; but, what if you don't have any? By excavating a hole in the ground and setting a container on the bottom, you can draw moisture from the soil.

Put a small weight (such as a rock) in the middle of the plastic cover to create a dip in the middle and seal the hole to prevent moisture from escaping.

Water condenses on the cover and drips into the bucket as it evaporates from the ground up. Obviously, this is not the quickest method of obtaining drinkable water, so try not to forget to bring some.

In an emergency, keep this strategy in mind, though: a box's side and a couple different kinds of plastic covers.

CHAPTER 4
Making Fire

Start of a fire

The ability to make a fire is a crucial survival skill. Fire is beneficial for

1. Warming up
2. Heating up water
3. Drying soaked clothing
4. Keeping some animals and insects at bay
5. To indicate where you are
6. Cooking

Always carry two different fire-starting techniques with you.

Setting up a Fire

Tinder, kindling, and logs are the three forms of fuel used to construct a standard campfire. Once the pile of tinder material has started to burn, it is rather simple to start the remainder of the fire—first with kindling (large sticks), then with logs.

Gather dry wood, start by scanning the evergreen trees' base for dead branches. To make tinder, take the smallest branches and chop them into tiny pieces with a knife or your fingers.

Dead grass, dried moss or fern, leaves, or a strip of fabric from your shirt's tail are all suitable sources of tinder since they can burn quickly.

Make a tiny circle of dry twigs into a teepee with your tinder in the center. Once it starts to burn, gradually add bigger and bigger pieces of wood to your fire. Before moving on to a larger piece of wood, always make sure the fire is burning freely. Don't let this fire go out once it starts burning. In addition to provide warmth and safety, it can serve as a signal to anyone looking for you.

Tinder

Numerous mosses, grasses, and other thin, fibrous things that ignite easily are sources of good tinder. Dryness is required. Gather flimsy-looking objects while hiking and save them in your shirt pocket since body heat quickly dries them off.

Here are some excellent places to find tinder that will fire in almost any circumstance:

- A cat with nine tails. This plant's enormous bulb at the top has enough "fluff" to ignite numerous fires.
- A particular species of fungus that burns exceptionally effectively is what causes the huge, black, lumpy growths on the sides of birch trees. Each lump has an interior color ranging from orange to brownish and can be lit with a spark to produce a lovely coal. Fire may be moved around by using this substance as well.
- In sandy soils, low-lying, gnarled pine trees and shrubs accumulate incredible volumes of sap. It becomes incorporated into the wood, making it extremely combustible. You should select dead branches in particular as they are full of sap and even a small piece can be utilized to ignite numerous fires. Only a strong spark will light up shavings of this kind of wood. A little bit is often enough.

Pocket lint has a high flammability. All it takes is a spark. If you end up stranded in the bush, you can choose from a variety of tinder that is simple to create. Cotton balls and dryer lint, for instance, both function effectively, especially when combined with Vaseline. As much dryer lint or cotton balls as will fit should be mashed and used to soak up the liquid after the Vaseline has been heated (either in the microwave or in a skillet on the stove) until it becomes liquid.

Until they are needed, these can be stored in a plastic bag, a piece of aluminum foil, an Altoids-style container, or any other compact container.

Fire Construction in the Snow

Although it can be a little challenging, if you stick to these fundamental guidelines, you'll succeed.

- Most fires quickly warm the area around them, but when there is wind, the majority of the heat is carried away. Additionally, a fire in the wind will use nearly twice as much wood. Choose a location to make your fire that is protected from the wind and weather.

- Gather all of your wood at once, and then arrange it according to size so you can quickly locate the proper piece when you need it.

- Even though wood is covered in snow, it may still be dry enough to burn, especially if the snow is light and fluffy, which indicates that it has less moisture.

- Break a stick to check the interior for moisture. It most likely is if it fractures. However, that snapping sound you hear when hiking after a winter rain could be ice. If so, you'll need to search for dry wood in safe spots, such as hidden beneath dense vegetation or inside the hollow of an old tree stump.

- Take wood samples from various locations on your property. Keep track of the kind of wood you find so you can return to those areas for more of the excellent stuff.

- It can take a long time to start working with wet or damp wood. You should always carry a fire starter with you because of this. Most outdoor sports shops, army-navy stores, and convenience stores in remote areas provide fire starters. Look for petroleum-based tablets, sawdust- and wax-filled balls of wax, and tubes of fire ribbon.

- As previously said, you can also make your own tinder out of cotton balls or laundry lint.
- Toilet paper barely burns for a second, thus there is no point in using it as tinder.
- Birch bark and pine needles are excellent fire starters. Search for fallen stumps.
- Fuel from a stove might give your fire the boost it needs to start. Never add fuel to a fire after it has been lit. Then light a match, and then back away!
- To build a fire on firm ground, dig a hole if the snow isn't too deep. If the snow is particularly thick and completely covers the ground, compact it so that it creates a tiny depression with a firm, hard platform in the center. After that, place a layer of wood on the snow before building your fire on top of it. Otherwise, your fire will become buried in the snow and extinguish before it ever starts.

TYPES OF FIRES

Lazy Man Fire

Starting a fire and keeping it going are both crucial. Always try to conserve energy if you're trying to survive. Don't waste time splitting firewood. Instead, add huge logs and branches to the fire and let it do the work. Move each log into the fire a little bit more as it burns. When you're not spending time chopping or sawing, it's astonishing how much wood you can gather.

Teepee Fire

Build it with standing wood lengths with kindling and tinder in the center. A reflecting oven needs a consistent, hot heat source, which the teepee fire provides. It needs a constant supply of lumber that is in the medium size range.

Pinwheel Fire

Lay tinder and kindling in the center of a pinwheel-shaped arrangement of one- to two- inch-diameter pieces of wood. A fry pan can be used to cook on this heat. Build a ring of rocks around it to support your fry pan.

Log Cabin Fire

Build a crosshatch pattern out of pieces of wood with a diameter of four to six inches. Allows for a lot of airflow and produces a quick supply of burning coals for roasting or grilling meat.

Keyhole Fire

When there are more survivors, the keyhole fire is a fantastic multipurpose fire. Construct a keyhole-shaped fire pit out of rocks. Then construct a teepee fire in the circular area. Create a wood cabin fire towards the conclusion. Once the log cabin fire's embers have died down, the tall flames of the teepee fire will provide illumination and warmth.

Fire at Dakota Pit

This fire is effective, consumes minimal fuel, and makes it simple to warm both you and your meal. It is simple to lean over for warmth or to put food or water over it to cook when it is confined in a hole. The second hole's purpose is to let oxygen reach the fire and keep it from being readily doused. The size of the pits you dig is the only factor that influences the magnitude of the fire.

Notably, this kind of fire is mostly utilized for warmth and does not produce much light. After deciding on a plausible location for the fire hole, remove a plug of dirt from the area and plant roots in the shape of a circle that is about ten or twelve inches in diameter. Save the plug and the dirt you removed for later replacement by continuing to dig straight down to a depth of about one foot.

1. The base of the fire chamber should be extended outward by a few inches in all directions to make room for longer pieces of fuel. As a result, fires can grow bigger and hotter since it takes less time and effort to cut firewood into manageable lengths.

2. Dig a six-inch-diameter air tunnel at an angle, starting approximately a foot from the fire pit's edge, so that it intersects with the fire pit's base. The result is a pit with a jug-like form at its base where firewood is placed. The purpose of the jug's neck acting as a form of chimney is to improve the draft and concentrate the heat of the fire into the tiny orifice.

3. Making the passageway for the fire hole is now necessary. The airway should be built on the side of the hole that faces the wind, so first establish the general direction of the wind.

4. Starting approximately a foot from the edge of the fire hole, dig your six-inch-diameter airway tunnel. Build the tunnel at an angle so that it meets the fire chamber's base. Make sure to keep both the loose dirt you remove and the plug containing the vegetation and roots.

5. Light the fire and partially fill the fire pit chamber with dry, flammable kindling. Add sticks gradually to the fire to maintain a strong, hot flame.

CHAPTER 5
Preparing for Bush-craft

Ropes and Knots

Basic understanding of knot-tying

The survivor will be helped to perform many vital tasks if they have a basic understanding of how to tie ropes and knots. Utilizing tried-and-true methods is necessary while making improvised equipment, shelters, packs, and safety gadgets.

A wrong knot can lead to injury, death, or useless improvised equipment.

Terminology for Ropes

1. Bend: In accordance with this regulation, a bend (also known as a knot) is used to tie two ropes together or to attach a rope to a ring or loop.

2. Bight: A bend or U-shaped curve in a rope is known as a bight.

3. Hitch: To secure a rope around a piece of wood, a pipe, or a post while still making it simple to untie, use a hitch.

4. Knot: Any tie or attachment created with a cord, rope, or line, including bends, hitches, and splices, is referred to as a knot. A knot is an interlacing of the components of bodies, such as cordage, generating a lump or knot. It is frequently utilized as a stopper to stop a rope from slipping through a gap.

5. Line: A line is a single thread, string, or cord (sometimes

referred to as a rope).

6. Loop: A loop is a fold or doubling of the rope that allows passage of another rope. A knot or a hitch creates a temporary loop. A splice or other long-lasting technique is used to create a permanent loop.

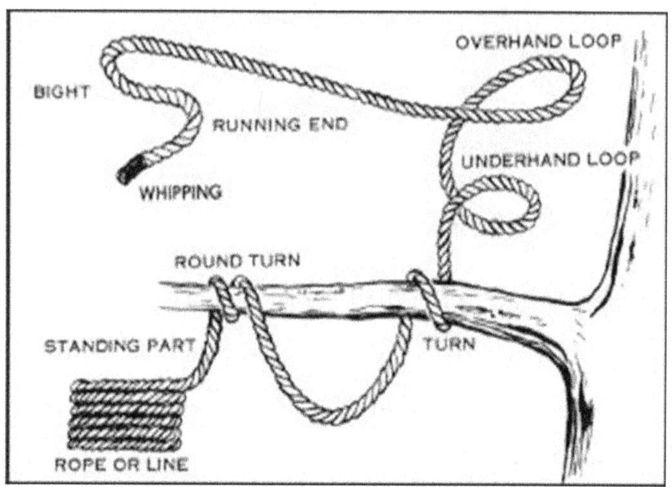

Rope and knot components

7. Overhand turn or loop: When the running end crosses the standing portion, an overhand loop is formed.

8. Rope: The strands of fiber that make up a rope (also known as a line) are twisted or braided together.

9. A Round Turn: The running end of a round turn exits the circle in the same general direction as the standing end, just like a turn.

10. Running End: The working or free end of a rope is known as the running end.

11. End Standing: With the exception of the running end, the standing end balances the rope.

12. Turn: A turn is the act of wrapping a rope around a certain structure, such as a post, rail, or ring, with the running end running counterclockwise to the standing end.

13. An underhand turn or loop: When the running end crosses beneath the standing part, an underhand turn or loop is created.

Shelter

Anything that shields a survivor from the dangers of the outside world is considered shelter. The information in this chapter explains how the environment affects the choice of a shelter site and variables that survivors must take into account before building a suitable shelter.

Also covered are the methods and procedures for building shelters for varying levels of protection.

Aspects of Shelter

Every condition that requires survival has a different location and type of shelter erected by survivors. When choosing a location, there are several factors to take into account. Survivors should take into account the time and effort needed to set up an acceptable camp, weather conditions, life forms (human, plant, and animal), topography, and time of day.

The environment should be protected as much as possible while utilizing the least amount of energy possible.

A. Time

It is not advisable to search for a place that would satisfy the needs for shelter that day in the late afternoon. If survivors wait until the very last minute, they could have to make do with subpar supplies in adverse circumstances.

They must continually consider how to meet their requirement for environmental hazard prevention.

B. Weather

When choosing a shelter location, weather is an important factor. It might be disastrous if the weather is not taken into account.

Temperature, wind, and precipitation are some significant meteorological variables that can affect the survivor's decision regarding the type of shelter and the site selected.

(1) Thermostat

Within a particular location, temperature variations might be significant. Setting up camp in a valley or other low spot in a cold climate might expose campers to low nighttime temperatures and wind-chill effects. It may be useful to position campsites to take advantage of the sun as colder temperatures can be found along valley floors, which are commonly referred to as "cold air sumps."

In order to increase warmth during the winter months and provide shade during the hotter months, survivors might construct their shelters in open locations. In some instances, a compromise could be necessary.

For instance, in many deserts, the daily high temperatures can cause water to freeze at the nighttime low temperatures. In these places, it is necessary to have protection from both heat and cold. To offer protection from the current temperature conditions, the type of shelter and its location should be chosen.

(2) Wind

Depending on the local temperature and the wind's speed, wind can be either a benefit or a drawback. By setting up camp atop knolls or spits of land, survivors can take advantage of the cool breezes and insect protection the wind offers throughout the summer or on hot days.

On the other hand, wind can become a nuisance or even a danger since blowing sand, dust, or snow can irritate the skin and eyes and harm clothing and equipment. Survivors should look for refuge locations that are shielded from the effects of wind-chill and drifting snow on chilly days or during the winter months.

(3) Precipitation

For survivors, the many types of precipitation, such as rain, sleet, hail, or snow, can be problematic. To prevent flash floods or mud slides caused by heavy rains, shelter locations should be away from large drainages and other low places.

If shelters are built in regions where there may be avalanche danger, snow can also be quite dangerous.

C. Living Things

When deciding on the campground and the kind of shelter that will be utilized, all living forms—plant, human and animal—must be taken into account. The "human" aspect could refer to the adversary or other parties that survivors want to avoid being discovered.

Certain variables must be taken into account for a shelter to be appropriate, especially if prolonged survival is anticipated.

1. Personal discomfort, disease, and harm can all be brought on by insect life. Survivors can lessen the amount of flying insects in their region by placing shelters on knolls, ridges, or any other location where there is a breeze or consistent wind. Mosquitoes, bees, wasps, and hornets can all be avoided by avoiding areas with standing water. Ants can be a significant issue; some species can aggressively defend their territory with painful stings, bites, or especially upsetting strong scents.

2. Animals of all sizes can be a concern, particularly if the camp is located close to their pathways or watering sites

3. It is best to stay away from standing dead trees and trees with dead branches. They could fall because of the wind, injuring or killing someone. When looking for a shelter, it's also important to stay away from poisonous plants like poison ivy and poison oak.

D. Terrain

Although they may not be as obvious as weather and animal life dangers, terrain hazards might be far more dangerous. Avoid avalanche, rock, dry streambeds, and mudslide zones. Either a visible route or a path of secondary vegetation, such as 1- to 15-foot-tall vegetation or other new growth that stretches from the top to the bottom of a hill or mountain, can be used to identify these regions.

Survivors shouldn't pick a shelter location at the base of a steep slope that might be prone to slides. Similar risks exist when camping at the base of a talus or scree slope. Before employing a rock overhang as a shelter, it is also important to ensure its safety.

Location

a. When choosing a shelter site, four conditions must be met.

1. The first is being close to sources of water, food, fuel, a signal, or a spot for recovery.
2. The second requirement is that the region be secure, offering built-in defense against environmental risks.
3. The third need is that there must be enough materials on hand to build the shelter. The "shelter" might even be there already in some circumstances. If survivors believe that shelter must consist of a manufactured framework with set dimensions and a cover made of parachute material or signal paulin, they severely limit their options. More suitably, survivors should think about utilizing shielded areas that are already there in the neighborhood. This simply broadens the range of what can be utilized as a survival shelter; it does not rule out shelters with a built framework and a parachute or other produced material covering.
4. The final requirement is that the location picked must be big enough and level enough for the survivor to lay down. For survivors, personal comfort is a crucial component. The physical and emotional well-being needed for restful sleep is provided by a suitable refuge. If survivors are to make wise decisions, they must get enough rest. As more time passes and there is a delay in rescue or return, their need for rest becomes more urgent. Survivors must choose a shelter's unique function before beginning construction.

CHAPTER 6
Survive a Nuclear Attack

The basis of a nuclear attack is an incident that presents a nuclear or radioactive hazard to the general public's health and safety, property, or environment. Nuclear or radiological emergency include.

- An emergency in a nuclear facility, such as a nuclear power plant

- An emergency involving a nuclear-powered vessel are examples of nuclear or radiological crises.

- A trucking accident involving the delivery of radioactive materials.

- An occurrence when radioactive material was misplaced, stolen, or discovered.

- A terrorist act that makes use of radioactive materials, such as a "dirty bomb" or an RDD (radiological dispersion device, which disperses radioactive material using ordinary explosives; this is NOT the same as a nuclear explosion).

- A nuclear blast. A nuclear detonation results in a nuclear blast. It involves the fusion and fission of atoms, which results in a powerful pulse or wave of heat, light, air pressure, and radiation. A sizable fireball is produced, and everything within of it vaporizes and is propelled upward to form a mushroom cloud.

The vaporized material in the mushroom cloud combines with

radioactive material from the nuclear bomb. As it cools and condenses, particles are created. Fallout is the term for the radioactive "dust" that has condensed and has since returned to Earth.

Wind currents may carry radioactive fallout over great distances, contaminating whatever it touches. The impact on people will vary depending on the magnitude of the bomb and their proximity to the explosion. Burns, flying debris, or the blast itself may all cause harm or even death.

The blast's powerful brightness might seriously harm your eyes. Radiation illness will develop in victims who are close to the blast site due to their high radiation exposure (called acute radiation syndrome, or ARS). Burns show up fast, but other symptoms may take many days to manifest.

A nuclear blast may result in two different forms of radioactive material exposure: internal exposure via contaminated air, food, and water, and external exposure from the blast and fallout. In a few of days or weeks, exposure to very high doses of radiation may result in death. Lower levels of exposure might cause cancer.

The level of damage brought on by a nuclear blast is not comparable to that of a nuclear power plant accident. A plume may include some radioactive material, but no fallout is created. The kind of accident, the radiation discharged, and the weather all affect the radiation risk in the immediate region. Local and plant officials would keep an eye on the situation and provide directions to the neighboring community in the event of an accident.

Do not get alarmed if you learn about an accident at a nuclear power plant in the area.

Radiation is not always released in accidents. In the case of a nuclear or radiological emergency, all governmental levels act. Depending on the location, nature, and scope of the emergency, the reaction begins at the local level and moves up to the state and federal levels.

Limiting your exposure to radiation is the key to surviving a radiation emergency. Utilize time, space, and protection.

Putting up a substantial shield can help you to block part of the radiation coming from the source.

Distance: The lesser your exposure, the farther you are from the source.

Less time spent close to the source equals less exposure. The terms "Alpha particles" and "Beta particles" refer to radiation types that can be blocked by either thin (for Alpha) or considerable (for Beta) shielding (for Beta).

A blast shelter is a shelter that provides defense against heat, fire, radiation, and blast pressure.

Any enclosed area that is sufficiently thick and dense to prevent or absorb the radiation emitted by fallout is referred to as a fallout shelter. Gamma rays are a piercing kind of radiation that should be shielded with a heavy, dense layer.

Ionizing radiation is radiation that has the potential to charge other atoms, including those found in human flesh.

Nuclear event: Detonation of a nuclear bomb that produces radioactivity and fallout and involves both fusion and fission.

Nuclear plant alerts—Unusual Event: a minor issue with no radioactive spill anticipated.

No action is required.

Alert: There is a little leak of radioactivity within the plant. No action is required.

Emergency in the site area: Sirens may sound. For advice and information, pay attention to the media.

Radiation leakage may be occurring outside the plant and away from the plant site. For advice and information, pay attention to the media. Pay close attention to directions. Radiation is the term for electromagnetic energy given off by radioactive materials.

Deposition of radioactive substances on surfaces is known as radioactive contamination. Radiation entering the body as a result of radioactive exposure. Patients who have been exposed are not always infected (e.g., X-rays).

An explosion and the emission of radioactivity are examples of a radiological event, which does not entail fission or fusion.

RDD—A "dirty bomb" or radiation dispersion device.

Roentgen and the rad are units of radiation that quantify the impact radiation has on an absorbent substance. The rem is a metric for the biological harm done to people.

Taking Care of Your Family and Yourself

The same way you would for any crises involving hazardous chemicals, be ready for these incidents:

- Enquire about the risks with the plant's management and local authorities. Learn more about the dangers to children, the chronically sick, and pregnant women. Ask about the locations of hazardous waste disposal sites and any other queries you may have regarding the handling and storage of materials in your neighborhood. Attend meetings where the public is informed.
- Become familiar with the local warning system and potential escape routes.
- Become familiar with the emergency procedures at the workplace, in nursing homes, schools, and childcare centers where you could find your family.
- Keep a disaster supply kit on hand.
- Follow your strategy for family communication. Clean Bomb vs. RDD It is thought that using an RDD—often referred to as

a "dirty nuke" or "dirty bomb"—by terrorists is far more plausible than using a nuclear explosive device. An RDD mixes radioactive material with a conventional explosive weapon, such a bomb. It is intended to disperse hazardous and non-lethal levels of radioactive material over a broad region. Terrorists are drawn to these RDDs because, in contrast to nuclear weapons, they are easier to create and employ.

Furthermore, it is simpler to access the radioactive elements used in RDDs than weapons grade uranium or plutonium and they are extensively utilized in agriculture, industry, research, and other fields.

The main goals of terrorist usage of an RDD are to instill fear in the minds of people and to harm the economy. Using certain equipment might expose users to radioactive elements and result in exposure. The number of fatalities and injuries from an RDD detonation may not be noticeably higher than from a conventional bomb explosion, depending on how quickly the area of the RDD detonation was evacuated and how well individuals were able to shelter in place.

The sophistication and size of the conventional bomb, the type of radioactive material used, the quality and quantity of the radioactive material, and the local meteorological conditions— primarily wind and precipitation—would all affect the size of the affected area and the degree of destruction caused by an RDD.

During cleaning activities, the impacted area can be closed to the general public for a while.

While the existence of an explosive blast will be clear right away, radiation won't be detected until skilled individuals and specialized equipment arrive on the site.

Be extra careful whether you are inside or outside, at home or at work. It would be preferable to presume radioactive contamination has already happened and take the necessary safety measures, especially if you're in an urban area or close to other potential terrorist targets. You want to prevent or restrict exposure, just as with any radiation. This is especially true when breathing in radioactive dust that is a byproduct of the explosion.

If there is visible dust or other toxins in the air where you are seeking shelter (inside or outside), breathe through the fabric of your shirt or coat to reduce your exposure.

Even if you are able to avoid breathing in radioactive dust, being close to the radioactive particles may expose you to some radiation.

If there is an explosion or radioactive leak inside, leave right once and find a secure shelter to hide. In contrast, if you are:

Outdoors

Find interior safety as soon as can in the closest undamaged shelter. If there is no suitable shelter nearby, cover your mouth and nose and retreat as quickly as it is safe upwind, away from the blast's site.

Then, locate suitable shelter as quickly as you can. Pay attention to any official instructions and obey them.

Indoors

If you have the time, shut windows, vents, fireplace dampers, exhaust fans, and clothes dryer vents. Also, switch off the ventilation and heating systems. Take your battery-operated radio and emergency preparedness equipment to your shelter room.

Find shelter right away, ideally underground or within a structure, and keep as much space and thick shielding as you can between you and any potential radioactive material outside. To lessen radioactive particle penetration, use duct tape to seal any gaps around windows and outside doors. Plastic sheets are ineffective as a blast against radioactivity or the effects of a nearby explosion.

Pay attention to any official instructions and obey them. Nuclear Warfare (recommendations from the World Health Organization)

If the Blast Is Close to You When it happens

- To avoid harming your vision, turn away, shield your eyes, and shut your eyes.
- Kneel down on the ground with your hands supporting your body.
- Remain flat until the two shock waves and the heat have subsided.

If the Blast Occurs While You Are Outside

- Use an item of clothing, such as a scarf, handkerchief, or other piece of fabric, to cover your mouth and nose.
- In a well-ventilated place, brush, shake, and wipe your clothing to remove any dust; but, while doing so, keep your mouth and nose covered.
- Head for a shelter, cellar, or other subterranean space, ideally one that is distant from the wind's direction.
- Take off your clothes since it can be polluted. If at all possible, get dressed, wash your hair, and take a shower before entering the shelter. If You Are Currently in a Basement or Shelter
- Shut off ventilation systems and lock doors or windows until the fallout cloud has gone.
- Cover your mouth and nose with a face mask or other material (such as a scarf or handkerchief). Unseal the doors and windows to let some air in once the fallout cloud has gone.
- Remain inside until the authorities deem it safe to go.
- For information and suggestions, tune in to the neighborhood radio or television. Authorities may order you to remain in your shelter or to leave the area for a safer location.
- Use a moist towel to cover your mouth and nose if you absolutely must go outside.
- Consume food and water that have been saved. Never

consume fresh food from the area or water from untreated water sources.

- Treat any open wounds you have on your body with care.
- If you've Been Told to Leave
- Keep an eye on the radio or television for updates on evacuation routes, makeshift shelters and best practices.
- Lock up the house, secure the windows, and switch off the heater, vents, and air conditioning before you leave. Shut the dampers and fireplace.
- Bring emergency supplies (such as a flashlight and extra batteries, battery-operated radio, first aid kit and manual, emergency food and water, nonelectric can opener, essential medicines, cash, credit cards, and sturdy shoes).
- Keep in mind that some of your neighbors, particularly young children, the elderly, and individuals with disabilities, may need special help.
- Immediately seek refuge in an emergency shelter. Your school-age children will get care there. Don't go running after them.

Accident at a nuclear power plant

- If you hear rumors of an accident, keep an eye on local media for updates and guidance.
- Unless otherwise ordered, bring family members and pets indoors and lock all windows and doors. When you're outdoors, keep your mouth and nose covered.
- Enter a lower-level inner room and lock all the doors and windows. Turn off the heating, fans, and air conditioning. Vent covers. Shut the fireplace's dampers.
- If authorities order an emergency evacuation, be ready to comply. Think about your neighbors who have unique needs.

When the Threat Is Over

- Potassium iodine, if taken soon enough after exposure, can block thyroid uptake of radioactive iodine and prevent thyroid cancer and other thyroid problems caused by inhaling or ingesting radioactive iodine.

- Avoid using foods from the garden or milk from nearby animals until they are approved by local authorities. The state has the authority to decide whether to utilize and provide potassium iodine to the community. Before using potassium iodine from your pack, seek the go-ahead from local health officials or emergency management staff. Pulse of Electromagnetic An electromagnetic pulse (EMP), a high-density electrical field, may be produced by a nuclear bomb detonated in or above the earth's atmosphere in addition to other effects. Similar to a bolt of lightning, an EMP has a stronger, quicker, and shorter duration.

Electronic equipment linked to power sources or antennas may sustain severe damage from an EMP. This comprises ignition systems for vehicles or airplanes, computers, electrical appliances, and communication systems. There might be anything from a slight disruption to major component burnout.

Within 1,000 miles of a high-altitude nuclear explosion, most electronic equipment may be impacted. Short-antenna battery-operated radios would often not be impacted. While the majority of individuals are unlikely to be harmed by an EMP, those who have pacemakers or other implanted electronic equipment may be.

The Consequences It will be exceedingly difficult to make future plans with all that fallout in the sky. If the Rule of Seven is not followed by the radiation decrease, you are either in a hot area or are being exposed to reactor fallout. Simple is the rule of seven: The radiation should be one tenth its initial value after seven hours, one hundredth after seven more hours, and so on.

You must move if the opposite is true.

You will have proof that a nuclear winter has begun at this point. Now, survivors must be housed in shelters. If they were in a target area, those without shelters would have ingested fatal quantities of radiation.

- If you decide to evacuate, measure your radiation exposure every 10 minutes. Read your dosimeter every hour if you have one. Record these readings in a log.
- You may have to take a measurement outdoors if you're in a shelter and don't have a remote probe for your radiation meter. Limit the length of your trip as much as you can. Take a number of readings in the area surrounding your shelter. Register each reading in a log.
- Clean up whatever you brought inside your shelter.

CHAPTER 7
Natural Disaster

The Basics of Earthquakes

Severe earthquakes and their catastrophic aftershocks are among the nature's most terrifying and destructive events. An earthquake is a sudden, violent shaking of the earth that is brought on by underground rock breaking and shifting as it relieves tension that has built up over a long period of time.

The planet has been fashioned by the forces of plate tectonics for hundreds of millions of years as the enormous plates that make up its surface slowly move over, beneath, and past each other. The movement might sometimes be gradual.

When this happens, the plates cannot release collected energy because they are locked together. The plates release when the energy builds up enough. If the earthquake takes place in a populous location, it might result in several fatalities, serious injuries, and significant property damage.

There is some earthquake danger in each of the 50 states and the five U.S. territories.

Every season of the year is susceptible to earthquakes.

The Lingo

Making changes to a building's interior and exterior to make them earthquake-resistant The area on the ground just above the earthquake's epicenter is called the epicenter.

An earthquake's energy (magnitude) is measured using the Richter scale, a 1–10 scale.

The Mercalli Scale is a scale used to gauge the strength of an earthquake's shaking. A scale-1 earthquake is minor and has little impact. A scale-12 earthquake results in almost complete devastation.

Tectonic plates are the outer plates of the earth that are moving in relation to one another.

Fault: A crack in the crust of the earth along which movement may occur, resulting in an earthquake.

The process of liquefaction, which occurs when saturated soil acts like liquid during an earthquake and causes catastrophic damage to buildings

An aftershock is a smaller earthquake that occurs in the same region as the first one.

Preparing for the Earthquake: Self and Family Protection

- Make structural changes, such as additional bracing, bolts for the sill plate or foundation, or hold-downs to anchor walls to foundations.
- Use angle bracing and structural straps to secure the chimney.
- Correct faulty wiring. Connect flexible utility lines.
- Install flexible connections and secure fuel tanks to the ground or floor.
- Use sturdy strapping to anchor large appliances like the furnace and refrigerator to wall studs.
- Use strong strapping or metal plumber's tape to firmly fasten the water heater.
- Keep breakables and bulky items on lower shelves.

- Strengthen ceiling fan and light fixture attachments.
- Mount shelves, frames, and mirrors on the walls.
- Select a different exit from each space.
- Run drills with your loved ones and colleagues.

The Earthquake

- Debris from crumbling buildings and falling items are the main causes of injury.
- If in a secure place, beneath a sturdy piece of furniture like a bed or desk, or against an interior wall, seek shelter immediately. • If you are in bed, remain there until the shaking stops.
- Steer clear of areas with windows, outside doors, or porous walls.
- Remain inside until the trembling stops.
- Remain where you are until the shaking stops if you are outside. Get into a crouch and shield your face and head with your arms.
- Get away from structures, fuel storage facilities, and electricity lines.
- Avoid entering any surrounding buildings.
- If you're driving, stop far from overpasses, gasoline tanks, utility poles, trees, and other obstructions.
- Press the panic button.
- Remain inside the car.

If you are buried in debris, create a breathing gap so you can escape.

- Avoid using lighters or matches.
- Remain motionless to prevent stirring up and inhaling dust.
- Use a handkerchief or piece of clothing to cover your mouth and nose.
- Tap on a wall or pipe to signal. Aftershocks are to be anticipated.

- Recognize the potential for floods and tsunamis. For example, in the "big one" anticipated along the Wasatch Fault, some experts estimate the Great Salt Lake could tilt and splash up against the west side of the Wasatch Mountains, killing thousands. If you are in a low region close to a huge body of water, move to higher ground. Local flooding danger may also rise due to liquefaction and dam damage. Tsunamis are a possibility in coastal locations. Get to a higher location.

- Enter damaged structures cautiously, ideally after authorities have checked the walls, ceilings, and foundation for shifting and structural soundness.

- Close the main gas valve if there is structural damage or if you smell gas.

- Turn off the power and have any shorts in your circuits tested.

- Follow the advice and information provided by the media.

- Keep clear of fallen power wires.

- If the pipes are damaged, turn off the main water valve within the house. Get outside if you smell gas. Turn off the gas main if you haven't already. Inform the Gas Company or authorities of any leakage.

- Before using the toilet, inspect the sewage pipes for damage.

- Carefully open cabinets.

- Clean up combustible spills.

- If at all feasible, get an expert to inspect the home for structural issues.

- Be ready to flee if necessary.

The Consequences

After an earthquake, it's important to reflect. To allow officials time to clean up and make urgent repairs, stay off the streets. You'll undoubtedly feel aftershocks, and they might be very strong.

Use this time to evaluate the damage and learn more about the earthquake's magnitude. Whether or whether you should set up a tent outside your house depends depend on how badly damaged it is. In either scenario, it is advisable to remain nearby to preserve the home's contents.

- Check for injuries and provide first assistance.
- Tune in to local stations on your battery-operated or vehicle radio for authoritative information.
- Look for any flames.
- Stay away from damaged structures since walls might still fall down.
- Turn off the gas, electricity, and water if you believe there has been damage.
- Only use the phone in genuine emergencies. Keep the lines accessible in case of emergency.
- If the water is off, you may utilize water from canned veggies, water heaters, toilet tanks (apart from those with additives), and melting ice cubes.
- Before flushing the toilet, check the sewage pipes.
- Look for damage to chimneys and record any cracks you find. If you can, try to do this from a distance.
- Use food from your freezer if the power is off to prevent spoilage. (Foods will remain frozen for 48 hours in a freezer that is fully stocked.)
- Resist the urge to travel. Maintain unobstructed passageways for emergency vehicles.
- When walking over debris, wear shoes.
- Anticipate aftershocks.
- When moving broken items, use thick gloves.

The insurance adjuster must be contacted, and announcements regarding government help and other victim assistance should be listened to.

You can be eligible for aid from the Red Cross as well as federal, state, and local organizations, depending on the extent of the damage. These organizations' top priorities will be rescuing stranded individuals and providing critical care. It won't be possible to build up a food distribution plan until that is finished.

What to do:

- Document the extent of the damage surrounding your property using a camera that takes still photos or video if you have one.
- List the damage, and include the serial numbers of any damaged equipment.
- Maintain your locality. Try to contact law police if you observe looters in your area.

Warning of Tsunamis

Tsunami warnings come in two varieties: international and regional.

The seismic wave produced by an earthquake, which usually precedes the tsunami, will reveal the location and intensity of the earthquake. A tsunami wave is nearly always anticipated to accompany an earthquake that occurs at sea.

The good news is that earthquakes are quickly detected since they move considerably more quickly than a tsunami wave, enabling time for a warning to be given. Special early warning buoys that are positioned out at sea can also keep an eye on the approaching tsunami.

While in principle this is acceptable, it is certain that the tsunami wave will approach faster and with more energy when an undersea earthquake occurs near to the coast. Most of the world's seas currently have early tsunami warning systems in place.

There won't be any other warning than the ground trembling for certain individuals. Those who follow their instincts at their core will survive, while those who don't will die.

Plan of Evacuation

Your local emergency agency will have prepared preparations for persons who reside in an earthquake or tsunami high-risk region. Determine what they are. Recognize the effects of a tsunami on your house, office, or place of employment. Learn which structures can resist the worst tsunami wave and where they are located.

Where is the nearest higher ground, and how quickly can you reach there with your family? Plan for the whole family since you can be dispersed throughout the workday.

The position should be at least 100 feet above sea level and at least two miles inland from the ocean. In as little time as possible—ideally under fifteen minutes—you should be able to go to your secure location. You should be able to go to your place of safety in the dark and during bad weather. Make sure your emergency kit is prepared and easily accessible.

Determine the required response time by calculating the distance between your place of residence and place of employment from the coast. Have the family practice driving, running, or walking to the closest safe area.

Plan a path of escape that won't be obstructed by panicked people. In the course of a typical day, these precautions may seem a little excessive, but even just one time of practice can significantly improve your odds of surviving a tsunami.

Ensure that your family's emergency plan is understood by all members. The specific duties and what each of you will do in the event of an emergency should be discussed. Make a point of coming back together when the tsunami has passed. Whether you're visiting a region at danger from a tsunami, find out if your accommodations have an evacuation plan, and again, be aware of the approved escape route.

Similarly, anybody without an evacuation plan who stay in their houses or near to the coast and ignore the warning noises will almost certainly die. The shaking of the earthquake alone should be enough to make you stop and ponder, even in isolated locations where no alert has been issued or heard. The first thing to keep in mind is that you cannot escape a wave that you can see coming toward the coast.

Second, you risk death or serious injury because of the wave's weight of rocks, trees, automobiles, and construction debris. The only thing you need to do is avoid the wave. As much as you can, ascend. It is essential to emphasize this. You should stop what you're doing as soon as a tsunami warning is issued or is audible, and move to higher ground.

You can get guidance from your local emergency management offices on the safest path to safety and potential shelter locations. Tsunamis are frequently marked in nations where they frequently occur.

Safety Reminders

- Always be ready to leave right away if you live in an earthquake-prone location. First off, get to high ground or a safe distance from the coast if you sense an earth quake, even if there isn't a tsunami warning.

- Upon hearing a tsunami warning, take the same action; however, be careful to alert as many people as possible who are close, particularly the extremely young and old. A huge tsunami creates noise, similar to an express train or an airplane. If there has been a predetermined evacuation spot and you have time, move to it.

- Following a catastrophe alert, panicked drivers may obstruct or block roadways. If necessary, leave your vehicle and go to foot to avoid waiting for the traffic to move. Keep in mind that highways are often constructed level by the shore, so if you need to gain height, utilize the neighborhood pathways.

- If you don't have enough time to relocate to higher ground, go to the top floor or the roof of the closest, strongest building.

- The majority of industrial enterprises and prefabricated dwellings will be carried away by the tsunami.
- If all else fails, climb a sturdy tree, ascend as high as you can, and hang on. Use your belt to firmly fasten yourself. (Many people in Thailand did this to survive.)
- A tsunami is a succession of waves, so wait until the situation is under control before going back to lower land.

Look around for anything that will float if you are unable to escape the tsunami wave and it is certain that you will be carried away. Look for a big floating piece of debris to utilize as a raft when the waves grow calmer. Ideal for the job is anything with a high buoyancy factor and good grip. Good swimmers are aware that they can stay afloat in the water by relaxing. However, tsunami seas are quite choppy, thus a flotation device is urgently needed.

Hurricane

A system of storms known as a tropical cyclone has a low pressure center and storms that may cause tornadoes, storm surges, strong winds, and heavy rain. As moist warm air rises and water vapor condenses, these storms form and intensify over warm waters.

Cyclones rotate counterclockwise in the Northern Hemisphere and clockwise in the Southern Hemisphere due to the Coriolis Effect (remember that from ninth-grade earth science?). Depending on their location and intensity or strength, cyclones are also known as tropical depressions, tropical storms, typhoons, cyclones, or hurricanes. When a tropical cyclone crosses over land, it becomes weaker.

The storm's full force falls mostly on the coast, where powerful gusts, copious amounts of rain, and storm surges all contribute to significant coastal flooding.

Winds are often less brisk in inland places, but severe floods from heavy rainfall is still a possibility.

A hurricane's central area of comparatively calm air is known as the Jargon Eye.

A hurricane is a big, revolving tropical weather system with winds that reach at least 74 mph.

Hurricane classifications

Storm surge: A localized increase in sea level brought on by a storm's powerful winds.

Hurricane/Tropical Storm Warning: Within the next 24 hours, hurricane/tropical storm conditions are anticipated.

Hurricane/Tropical Storm Watch: Within the next 36 hours, hurricane/tropical storm conditions might develop. For information, tune in to a NOAA weather radio or other media.

Storm tide is the result of combining the tide and storm surge.

A tropical storm is a group of well-organized, powerful thunderstorms with a well- defined circulation with top sustained winds of 39 to 73 mph.

How to Prepare Yourself and Your Family for a Storm

- Understand the hazards, escape routes, and safe haven sites in your area.
- Bring inside outdoor accessories like couches and awnings. Securely fasten heavy items. Near and tighten window shutters or cover windows with plywood or boards. Check your disaster supply box to make sure the radio and lights function and the batteries are fresh. Cut down and rid of any dead branches and any live branches that are too close to the home.
- Close all windows and doors to lessen vibration. To reduce and control flying glass, close draperies and curtains and tape

windows.

- Anchor or tie down mobile homes.
- Examine your insurance contract.
- Put gas in the vehicle and get ready to flee.
- For information, tune in to the NOAA weather radio or other media.
- If instructed to leave immediately.

When the Storm Hit

- Avoid going outside and stay indoors. If you have a safe room, enter it.
- Keep clear of floodwaters.
- Tornado watch is advised.
- Keep in mind that the storm is only halfway done if the "eye" is still there.

Following the Storm: Follow news reports for updates

- Don't enter until the location has been deemed safe.
- Check for damage with a flashlight, paying particular attention to gas, water, electrical, and appliance lines.
- Disconnect the gas main if you smell gas or flames. Turn off each circuit breaker separately (or unscrew individual main fuse).
- Keep clear of fallen power wires.
- Only make urgent phone calls.
- Only consume the local water if it has been deemed safe if the region has flooded. Food tainted by floodwaters should be thrown away.

The Consequences

Identifying the Damage

Once the storm has safely passed, one of your first actions will be to evaluate the damage. Use flashlights instead than matches, candles, or anything else with an open flame if it's still dark and you can't wait for morning since there can be gas leaks. What about your neighbors if you don't have gas at home? Why endure a storm just to have your home burn down soon after? It occurs.

Additionally, if you have young children or dogs, you should promptly wipe up any spilled medications, narcotics, or other potentially toxic substances. Outside, there is standing water and a lot of damp vegetation. There is also very definitely some dispersed debris. If at all possible, avoid going outside after dark, but if you must, go as quickly and safely as you can.

Never allow your kids to play in any standing water, not even when it is daytime. It may at the very least contain sewage or, worse, be concealing a broken electrical line, deadly sharp items, or an open hole in the earth.

Tornado

When a warm, humid air mass and a cold air mass collide, a powerful, spinning column of air is created, known as a tornado. The base of a cumulonimbus cloud above, as well as the ground below, is often in touch with the column, or condensation funnel cloud. Typically, a debris cloud surrounds the funnel's bottom.

Although they do occur overseas, tornadoes most often occur in the United States. A waterspout is a tornado over water. Although they may travel twice as fast or half as fast, tornadoes typically move at a pace of 30 miles per hour. The internal winds have a maximum speed of 300 mph.

A hundred-foot broad and kilometers long destruction path is possible. According to the damage they inflict, tornadoes are classified using the Fuijita (F) Scale or the Enhanced Fujita Scale (EF). An F0 can take some tree branches off and causes some damage, but it won't substantially harm buildings. A structure will be torn from its foundation and will sustain tremendous damage in an F5.

Tornadoes may hit suddenly, move quickly, and abruptly change directions. It is not essential to be aware of the prospective F grade. Take the necessary measures if you hear the warning or see the funnel.

A funnel cloud, which is often difficult to detect, a pitch-black sky with an unsettling greenish tint, and sizable dark low-lying clouds are all indicators of a tornado.

A measure for assessing tornado strength and damage is the Fujita scale.

Weather radar has detected or suggested the presence of a tornado. Take cover right away.

Tornado Watch: There is a chance of tornadoes. Keep an eye out for impending storms.

Keep an eye on the skies and listen to the NOAA weather radio or other media for updates. Before the tornado season, protect yourself and your family by finding or building a low, windowless, sturdy shelter.

Consider a secure room, the basement, a space beneath the stairs, a lower-floor internal corridor, or a closet.

- Locate or construct a low, windowless, sturdy structure to take cover in. Think of a closet on the lowest level, the basement, a secure room, an inside corridor, or a space beneath stairs.
- If your home is a mobile home, tie it down to prevent more damage but don't use it as a refuge.
- Become familiar with the local siren signals.
- Practice drills as a family.

When a Tornado is About to Occur

- Quickly take shelter. Flying debris is the main cause of injuries. Report any tornadoes you see.
- Keep away from windows to prevent flying glass fragments.
- Head to the inside of the basement, the internal room on the lowest level, or your allocated refuge. Stay away from corners, exterior walls, doors, and windows. Avoid standing directly below large appliances or furnishings that are on the floor above.
- Hide beneath a large table or other solid object. Use a mattress or thick blankets to protect yourself. Protect and cover your face and head.
- Head to the local tornado shelter if you live in a mobile home. If there isn't one or you're pressed for time, go to the basement or the lowest level of a substantial adjacent structure. If it's not feasible to do that, exit the mobile home and lay down in the closest dip in the ground, ideally a ditch or culvert.
- Stop and exit if you're in a car.
- Find a nearby low area or ditch.
- Don't ever crawl beneath a vehicle. Avoid being near automobiles
- Under a structure or with your arms, shield your head.
- Keep away from wooded regions.
- If you are not at home, take the above-mentioned safety measures
- Avoid using elevators.
- If you're at a mall or big gym: • Keep your distance from glass doors and windows.
- Drop to the bottom.
- Hide behind a door frame or crowd up against a building that may catch flying debris.

Following a tornado

- Don't enter a building until officials have inspected the walls, ceilings, and foundation for movement or cracking.
- If you smell gas, immediately close the main valve and dial the gas company.
- Turn off the power and get a professional electrician to check for circuit shorts.

Seasonal Storm

Winter storms are meteorological disturbances that bring together chilly temperatures and the precipitation that results from them (snow, sleet, ice, freezing rain).

These are typically wintertime occurrences, although they may also happen in the spring and the autumn. The impacts of precipitation, or the combined effects of precipitation and cold, are the main topic of this section. See the section below this one for heat and cold crises.

Winter storms may cause devastation:

- Traffic disruption and increased risk of accidents because to poor visibility, slippery roads, and deep drifts
- Cutoff of emergency response teams
- Increased risk of cold-related injuries
- Disruption in the movement and delivery of commodities and supplies, leading to a shortage of food, water, and medical supplies for people and animals (frostbite and hypothermia, exertion injuries and illnesses, and carbon monoxide poisoning)
- Collapse of structures, including as buildings and electrical lines, as a result of heavy, wet snowfall.
- Flooding in low lying places; • Avalanches in high locations (frequent in Alaska, Colorado, Utah, and certain other

mountain states);

Avalanche definition: A massive mass of snow or ice sliding down a mountainside.

A prediction that alerts people to a serious avalanche hazard is called an avalanche warning. A blizzard has winds of 35 to 44 miles per hour and fewer than 500 feet of visibility. Winds exceeding 45 miles per hour and no visibility are indicators of a severe snowstorm.

Blizzard Warning: For a period of three hours or more, there will likely be strong winds or gusts that reach 35 mph or higher, along with significant snowfall or blowing.

Frost or Freeze Warning: Expected temperatures below freezing.

Heavy Snow Warning: There will likely be a lot of snow, which will make travel hazardous.

Winter Storm Warning—Life and property are at danger due to an impending, probable, or major severe winter storm or dangerous winter weather.

Significant winter weather is anticipated during the next 12 to 36 hours.

How to Prepare Yourself and Your Family for a Storm

As part of general winter preparations, water should be drained from sprinkler lines, outdoor hoses, and interior valves that feed outdoor hose faucets. Outside valves should also be opened to drain water and enable ice to expand.

- Use heat tape or insulating sleeves to shield pipes.
- Insulate your attic and walls.
- Clear debris from rain gutters to promote drainage and prevent ice and snow buildup.

- Get ready for a power outage. Keep a catastrophe supply kit on hand. Keep a sufficient amount of heating fuel on hand.
- To prepare your house for winter, fix any roof damage and plug any tiny holes in the walls, particularly those near pipes and vents. Keep the weather-stripping on your doors and windows.
- Inspect the batteries in your carbon monoxide and smoke detectors.
- Hire an expert to clean your chimney, flues, and furnace.
- Maintain your snow removal tools.
- Winterizing your vehicle
- Maintain a full tank.
- Inspect and clean the battery terminals.
- Check the thermostat and antifreeze levels.
- Inspect the windshield wipers, defroster, heater, and add windshield washer fluid.
- Examine the exhaust setup.
- Switch to a lighter oil.
- Mount snow tires or all-weather radials.
- Keep a broom and an ice scraper in the vehicle.
- Keep an emergency kit in your vehicle.

After a Storm

- Dress in layers.
- Use insulation or an outside heat source to safeguard water lines. To avoid freezing, allow faucets to drip a little bit of water.
- Prevent drinking water from freezing in a vehicle
- Only use your car throughout the day and only if it's really essential.
- Stay on major thoroughfares.
- Go on a trip with a friend.

- Share your destination, plans, and travel details with someone.
- Bring a two-way radio or a mobile phone.
- If you become stuck in a snowstorm, pull over, switch on your warning lights, or secure a bright piece of cloth or tape to your antenna or window. You will lose engine heat by raising the hood, which might be a distress indication.
- For ventilation, open a window towards the downwind side.
- To avoid carbon monoxide poisoning, just run the heating and engine for 10 minutes each hour. Occasionally clean the exhaust of snow.
- Only turn on an overhead light while the car is operating.
- Huddle up and insulate as much as you can.
- Frequently switch positions and move about to warm up your body and prevent cramping.
- Take turns keeping an eye out for danger.
- Sip on liquids to prevent dehydration. Never consume snow or ice. It brings down body heat.
- Stomp an SOS into thick snow to send a signal after the storm passes, or burn motor oil for a smoke and fire signal if you are stuck.

Following a Storm

- Pay attention to the media for news and predictions.
- Research road conditions using telephone and Internet tools.
- Keep an eye out for any of your neighbors who may have special needs.

The Consequences

Examine the damage to your home and, if you can, take pictures. You may create short- term fixes to keep out the weather. You'll need plastic sheeting and duct tape.

What to do:

- Contact the utility companies and report any damaged gas, electric, or sewage lines.
- Contact your insurance provider.

CHAPTER 8
Terrorist/cyber attack

Terrorism is the use of force or violence against persons or property for purposes of intimidation, coercion, or ransom. Terrorists often use threats to:

- Create fear among the public.
- Try to convince citizens that their government is powerless to prevent terrorism.
- Get immediate publicity for their causes.

Threats of attacks, murders, abductions, hijackings, bomb scares, explosions, cyber-attacks (computer-based), and the use of CBRN and radioactive weapons are all examples of terrorism. Military and civilian government buildings, international airports, big cities, famous monuments, major public gatherings, water and food supplies, utilities, business hubs, and mass transportation networks are among the high-risk targets for terrorist attacks.

You would need to depend on neighborhood police, firefighters, and other authorities for guidance during a terrorist strike. Eventually, the reaction will include state and federal entities.

The Jargon

Chemical, biological, radiological, nuclear, and explosive (CBRNE) are the most probable weapons of mass devastation and terrorism; arson should be included.

A secondary device is one that is planned to go off after emergency services like the police, fire department, and ambulance have arrived or have collected in safe places.

The use of violence or threats of violence to forward an agenda or intimidate is known as terrorism. WMD stands for a weapon or agent that is intended to kill many people or significantly harm both infrastructure and property.

Safeguarding your family and yourself

You may get ready just as you would be ready for other crisis situations. FEMA recommends the broad rules listed below:

- Pay attention to your surroundings.
- Keep in mind that the following are potential targets: skyscrapers and high rises, bridges and tunnels, pipelines, harbors, landmarks of significance and religion, schools,
- governmental structures, churches, malls, computer networks and data systems, power systems, mass transit vehicles, and food and water supplies.
- If you feel uneasy or if anything doesn't seem right, get up and go.
- When traveling, use care. Be on the lookout for outlandish or strange conduct. Never accept packages from unidentified people. Never let your baggage sit unattended. You must notify the police or security staff as soon as you see any odd activity, suspicious or unattended shipments, or weird electronics.
- Find out where the emergency exits are in the buildings you often use. Make a plan for your escape in case of emergency.
- Be ready to live without the following services: power, telephone, natural gas, gas stations, cash registers, ATMs, and online transactions.

Work with the building's owners to make sure the following things are situated on each floor:

- A battery-powered, portable radio and additional batteries.
- A number of flashlights and additional batteries.
- A first-aid handbook and kit.
- Dust masks and hard helmets.
- Rope off risky locations using fluorescent tape.
- Report suspicious activity to 911 or your local law enforcement services number when the threat level is Orange or Red.
- Be prepared for obstructions, delays, and searches while entering public places.
- Be prepared for traffic restrictions and delays.
- Steer clear of busy locations or big crowds.
- Keep an eye on the news and be ready to flee or take cover.
- Avoid spreading rumors yourself or with others.

How to Respond to a Bomb Attack

IEDs pose a hazard to troops, but terrorist bombing operations often target large numbers of civilians. The majority of terrorist explosions occur in densely populated locations with little to no notice, and the results are invariably horrifying. Your first concern should be to leave the area if you find yourself close to a bomb detonation.

In the event that a second device is scheduled to go off after the rescue crews arrive, this enhances your odds of survival. Additionally, it lessens your exposure to any potentially harmful gasses, smoke, or dust that may be discharged as a consequence of the explosion. Many Americans who survived 9/11 have since passed away from malignancies that are believed to be linked to breathing in debris from the destroyed towers.

You are clearing the way for the rescue personnel to better help individuals who are seriously hurt and unable to move by transferring yourself to a secure location. If a bomb threat is issued, it is your responsibility to leave as quickly as possible. However, if a bomb goes off while you are inside a structure, find cover below a solid table or desk. When the immediate threat has passed and it is safe to do so, leave the building as soon as you can.

You are urged to utilize the stairs rather than the elevator since there may have been damage to the building's structural integrity (in some high-rise buildings, the elevator may be your only viable option).

- Don't stop to pick up items for yourself, make calls, etc.
- Help others out if you can.
- Once outdoors, retreat to a secure location and watch out for further dangers like glass or loose masonry falling on you.
- Keep moving until you reach emergency personnel or a location that is known to be safe.
- Secondary explosions may have been detonated in many instances; these are often intended to interfere with the rescue efforts.
- Although you may want to contact home, friends, or coworkers to see how they're doing, try to utilize text messages instead of phone calls. The networks are turned down after a significant tragedy because they are overwhelmed.
- Use whatever you have on hand to cover your mouth and nose to prevent inhaling dust or other dangerous substances. Remain calm if you are confined to a room or building or if your escape path is blocked. Let the dust settle before making any needless movements to allow you to see.

The likelihood of a severe fire following a bombing is low since most buildings are composed of concrete, although some furniture, particularly drapes, could be on fire. Water pipes could leak, and the building's structure might be broken or missing pieces. Follow these steps if you are trapped:

- If a fire is present and it is too large for you to handle, get away from it.
- Can you relocate to a safer area if your present location is dangerous?
- Check to see whether you're alone or if anybody else is close.
- Do you or anybody in your immediate family need emergency medical care?
- Use a flashlight, a whistle, or a yell to let others know where you are. Tap on pipes or radiators to create an echo throughout the building.
- Before making a decision, evaluate your circumstances.
- You want to leave the building as safely as you can.
- If you have to wait for rescue assistance, be patient and follow their instructions properly. It is sometimes difficult to defend oneself against bombs.
- You should wait for rescue assistance in your railway car unless you are in urgent danger.
- If you can, and it's safe to do so, open windows or doors. Doing so may lessen the severity and quantity of injuries caused by a potential secondary explosion.
- Attend to everyone who is hurt and give them comfort.
- If you are in danger and need to move, select which path to follow to the closest above- ground or subterranean escape, and call for anybody in the train car with medical expertise. It is not advisable to go down the track's edge since there are several dangers present, not the least of which is electricity that may not be turned off.

The Consequences

Around this time, even the government acknowledges that terrorists with foreign bases are attacking us.

As a consequence, those nationalities who reside on American territory will face persecution, creating a favorable environment for the recruitment of genuine terrorists. It will affect people across the world how Americans feel about terrorism. Some nations have residents who will treat Americans visiting there horribly.

Individuals who support terrorism may attack Americans who work with overseas humanitarian organizations. American-owned companies operating abroad will come under attack from local terrorist supporters and would-be terrorists. Self-storage lockers are encouraged to be used to keep weapons, ammo, explosives, narcotics, and other materials in many underground publications.

Numerous of these self-storage facilities will be subject to monitoring and raids by police forces. Those still in business will request that the prospective tenant's identification be confirmed. Steps to take:

- Look closely at the demographics of your community. You may wish to relocate or enhance your insurance coverage if you discover that a significant portion of the population is made up of citizens of the nation carrying out the terrorist raids.
- Listen to radio transmissions on shortwave originating from the nation that exports terrorists. Ask them if there are any particular locations or occasions they would want to target.

CHAPTER 9
Biological Attack

Emerging infections are those that have just surfaced, are rapidly expanding geographically, or pose a danger of expanding. They may be brought on by pathogens that were previously unidentified, by well-known pathogens that have spread to new areas or new people, or by pathogens that have just emerged.

Infectious disease diseases or resurgences may be caused by a variety of circumstances, such as the pathogen's natural development or direct effects of human activity. Urbanization, international air travel, poverty, armed conflict, and environmental excesses may all have a growth.

An emerging infectious disease needs both a susceptible population and the capacity to move quickly from one person to another in order to thrive. Many of these diseases begin to spread when they are transferred from animals to people. Influenza and HIV are two examples of this.

Acquired resistance to antibiotics and antivirals is a crucial element in the resurgence of infectious diseases. Scientists anticipate it to become worse since we've already seen it with TB, STDs, and other illnesses over the last several decades.

Pathogens and associated poisons are called "bioterrorism agents" when they are utilized by terrorists to kill and infect plants, animals, and even people.

These "germs" are often ones that are present in nature but have been altered to make them more virulent, resistant to drugs or vaccinations, or better able to spread across the environment and from person to person. Because they are cheap and available, biological weapons are appealing to terrorists. They are readily producible and undetectable when delivered.

The majority of bio agents need an incubation time. Without even the presence of the terrorist, they may wreak havoc and spread fear. The capacity to spread, fatality rates, probability of causing public panic, and necessary countermeasures are used to categorize pathogens and poisons that might be employed as bioterrorism agents into Class A, B, and C.

Category A agents are regarded as the worst (or the best, from the perspective of a terrorist) because they are easily transmitted from person to person and present the highest risk to national security due to their high mortality rates, capacity to cause panic, and difficulties in controlling their spread. Some nations have explored anthrax, botulism, plague, smallpox, tularemia, and viral hemorrhagic fevers like Ebola and Marburg for use in biological warfare.

In addition to those agents that are now regarded as emergent infectious concerns, such as SARS and drug-resistant TB, Category C contains bacteria that may have been created for spread. Wet or dry aerosol sprays, explosive devices, vectors, direct contact with carriers, introduction into our food and water, medicine contamination, or contact with germ-filled items may all be used to deliver bio weapons.

The lingo

- An antibiotic is a chemical that may inhibit or stop the growth of germs.
- An antiviral is a chemical that may inhibit or stop the growth of viruses.
- Pathogens and poisons might be employed as bioterrorism agents
- Contagious disease are disease that is spread by contact with an infected individual

- Disinfection: Cleaning that eliminates "germs."
- Dissemination: To disseminate widely or internationally.
- Eradication: The full elimination of disease brought on by the invasion of dangerous organisms is an infectious disease.
- The incubation period is the interval between exposure to the germ and the onset of symptoms in the patient.
- Isolation—Removes sick, infectious diseases from the broader populace.
- Microorganisms are microscopic creatures that may either cause or not cause disease.
- Pathogens are microorganisms that cause disease, such as parasites, viruses, and bacteria.
- People who may have been exposed to an infectious disease but are not yet sick are separated in quarantine.
- A toxic chemical generated by bacteria is called a toxin.
- A preparation of a pathogen that is disease-free but has been weakened or killed a vaccine encourages the formation of antibodies.
- An organism that spreads germs that cause disease from one organism to another is a vector.
- The ability of a germ to cause disease is known as virulence.
- Disease diseases that may infect people are transmitted as zoonosis.

Protecting Your Family and Yourself against a Biological Threat

There has been a great deal of hardly understandable worry on the part of the public and the government over bioterrorism and new illnesses. A pandemic is a terrible idea because of how many people it would kill. In the present day, a never-ending supply of films in the Dawn of the Dead and Andromeda Strain genres has fuelled that anxiety.

Let's be reasonable and doable about this. Emerging illnesses and biological warfare are both just infectious diseases, and there are conventional, everyday methods of decreasing your risk of contracting either one:

- Always wash your hands after using the bathroom and particularly before and after handling meals.
- Vaccinate yourself. Maintain the efficacy of your child's and your own vaccinations. Get the vaccinations advised for your location if you want to travel.
- Only use antibiotics and antivirals when necessary. Follow the instructions precisely. If you feel better, don't stop taking them before you should.
- If you feel ill or have cold symptoms, stay at home. If you have a fever, diarrhea, or nausea, avoid going to work. If your children exhibit these symptoms, don't send them to school.
- Properly prepare the meal. Keep the kitchen countertops and other surfaces clean. Refrigerate leftovers right away.
- Clean up your home's "germiest" spaces, the kitchen and the bathroom.
- Engage in discreet sex.
- Avoid sharing towels, drinking glasses, combs, razor blades, toothbrushes, and dining utensils.
- Travel with discretion and consideration. Nobody likes to travel in a taxi or fly in an airplane cabin with a sick person.
- Maintain your dogs' health. Maintain proper pet hygiene and nutrition. Ensure that they get their vaccinations on time. If they get ill, see a veterinarian.
- Be sure to heed the authorities' instructions in the case of an outbreak or act of biological terrorism. They could advise you to take cover. You can be subjected to a decontamination procedure. You could end up in quarantine.
- Follow the advice and information provided by the media.

- For further information, get in touch with your state and local health agencies. You may avoid infectious diseases and prevent their spread with a little common sense and the right safety measures.

When a Biological Threat Occurs

When you start experiencing signs of a disease brought on by agent exposure, it might be the first sign of an assault. Follow these recommendations if a biological hazard is present:

• Public health professionals may not be able to promptly advise you on what to do in the case of a biological assault. Finding out precisely what the condition is, how to treat it, and who is at risk will take some time. For official news and information, however, such as the indications and symptoms of the disease, risk zones, if drugs or vaccinations are being delivered, and where you should go to the doctor if you get sick, you should instead watch TV, listen to the radio, or search the Internet.

- Run away as soon as you become aware of a strange or suspicious chemical.
- Guard yourself. Layers of air-filtering clothing over your mouth and nose will still enable you to breathe. Examples include a towel, handkerchief, or two to three layers of cotton clothing like a t-shirt. If not, using multiple layers of tissue or paper towels might be helpful.
- There may be instances when you should think about using a face mask to prevent coming into touch with infectious germs if individuals around you are ill or to lessen the transmission of germs if you are ill yourself.
- Remove your clothing and personal belongings and bag them if you have been exposed to a biological agent. For the proper disposal of hazardous materials, according to the regulations.
- Wash your hands well in soapy water, and then put on fresh

clothing.

- Make a call to the authorities and go to the hospital. You might be told to avoid social situations or even placed in quarantine.
- It's crucial to be cautious if a family member is ill.

However, don't presume that you need to visit an emergency department at a hospital or that any ailment is related to the biological assault. Many common ailments have overlapping symptoms.

- Maintain cleanliness and excellent hygiene to prevent the transmission of germs, and see a doctor as needed.
- Ask yourself whether you belong to the group or region that the authorities consider to be under risk.
- If you are in the category deemed to be at risk and your symptoms match those mentioned, you should seek emergency medical assistance right once.
- Comply with advice from medical professionals and other public health authorities.
- Be prepared to get medical assessment and treatment if the disease is communicable. You can get advice to avoid social situations or perhaps be placed in quarantine.
- Be prepared to receive medical evaluation and treatment for non-contagious diseases. It might be prudent to avoid large gatherings of people in the event of a biological emergency or epidemic.

CHAPTER 10

Preppers Natural Medicine

Calligonum comosum abal

One of the few shrubby plants that may be found in the shaded deserts is the abal. This plant has branches that resemble the wisps of a broom and grows to a height of around 1.2 meters. In the early spring, the stout, green branches are covered in a profusion of flowers.

Habitat and Distribution: This plant may be found in every climatic zone amid desert waste and brush. Most of the North African desert is home to it. As far east as the Rajputana Desert in western India, it may also be found on the sands of the Middle East's deserts.

The plant's outward look might not suggest that it would be helpful to a survivor, yet its fresh flowers, which bloom in the spring, are edible. In the regions where it is located, this plant is widespread. This plant has been shown to be very nutritious because to its high sugar and nitrogenous content.

Acacia

The farnesiana acacia

A spreading, often small tree with spines and alternating compound leaves is an acacia. Each of its leaflets is rather little. Ball-shaped, brilliant yellow, and very fragrant describe its flowers. It has whitish-gray colored bark. It produces pod-shaped, dark brown fruits.

Acacia grows well in regions that are open and sunny. It may be found in all tropical

areas.

There are over 500 different species of acacia. Although several species of these plants

may be found in the hotter and drier parts of America, they are particularly common in Africa, southern Asia, and Australia.

Young leaves, flowers, and pods are all edible, either fresh or cooked.

Agave

A center stalk is surrounded by enormous clusters of these plants' thick, fleshy leaves that are carried near to the ground.

Agave species

The plants only have one blossom before dying. They generate a huge bloom stem.

Agaves enjoy dry, open spaces for their preferred habitat. They may be found in the western deserts of the United States, Mexico, and most of Central America as well as the Caribbean and the Caribbean Islands.

Edible components Both the blossom buds and the flowers are edible. Before consuming them, boil them.

Caution

Some people get dermatitis after ingesting the juice of some species.

Almond.

Cut the enormous flower stem and save the liquid for drinking. Some species have leaves that are highly fibrous. To make fibers for weaving and producing ropes, pound the leaves. The tips of the leaves on the majority of species feature thick, pointy needles. Use them for hacking or stitching.

Some species' sap has a component that makes it good for soapmaking.

Amygdala Prunus

The almond tree, which may reach a height of 12.2 meters, grows a peach tree. The unripe, twisted raw almond fruit grows in bunches and resembles a peach. The skin of the stone (the almond itself) is thick, dry, and shaggy.

Almonds may be found in all climatic zones in the desert scrub and waste, evergreen scrub forests in temperate regions, and tropical scrub and thorn forests. Aside from the semi- desert regions of southern Europe, the eastern Mediterranean, Iran, the Middle East, China, Madeira, the Azores, and the Canary Islands, the almond tree may also be found there.

Edible components The ripe almond nut is revealed when the mature almond fruit breaks apart lengthwise along the side. By simply splitting up the stone, you may quickly get the dry kernel. Like other nuts, almond meats are rich in nutritional content. Gather them in large numbers and shell them to use as additional food for survival. Almonds are a relatively long-term food source. The outer shell of the kernel is removed during the boiling process, leaving only the white meat.

These 90 to 150 centimeter tall plants, which are common weeds in many parts of the world, belong to the Amaranth Amaranths species. The leaves on amaranth are all alternately simple. On the stems, there may be a hint of red. At the top of the plants, they produce dense clusters of tiny, greenish flowers. In weedy species, their seeds may be brown or black, while in domestic species; they may be light in color.

Habitat and Distribution: Amaranth can be found growing as weeds in crops, along roadside ditches, and disturbed waste areas all over the world. Some parts of amaranth have been cultivated as a grain crop and a garden vegetable around the globe, particularly in South America.

All parts are edible, but you should remove any sharp spines from some of them before eating. Alder plants' young plants or growing tips make a delicious vegetable. Eat the young plants raw or simply boil them. Their seeds are incredibly nourishing. To collect the seeds, shake the tops of alder plants. Consume the seeds uncooked, boiled, flourized, or popped like popcorn.

Polar willow

The Arctic Salix

The tundra is home to the arctic willow, a shrub that never grows taller than 60 centimeters and clusters into dense mats.

North American tundras are a frequent habitat for the arctic willow. both Asia and Europe. In certain hilly locations of temperate climates, you may also locate it.

Edible components In the early spring, you can gather the tender, succulent young shoots of the arctic willow. Remove the new shoots' outer bark and consume the interior raw. The young underground shoots of any of the various species of arctic willow can also be peeled and eaten raw. One of the richest sources of vitamin C is young willow leaves, which have 7 to 10 times as much as an orange.

CHAPTER 11
Making Energy

Renewable energy

Utilizing the sun, wind, water, heat from the Earth, and plants, renewable energy employs energy sources that nature continuously replenishes. These fuels are converted into useful forms of energy using renewable energy technologies, most often electricity, but sometimes heat, chemicals, or mechanical power.

Reasons to Use Renewable Energy

Fossil fuels are what we largely utilize today to heat and power our houses and to fuel our automobiles. Although using coal, oil, and natural gas to satisfy our energy demands is practical, there is a finite amount of these fuels available on Earth. They are being used far faster than they are being made. They will eventually run out. Additionally, the United States will retire a large portion of its nuclear capacity by 2020 due to safety concerns and issues with waste disposal. In the meanwhile, it is anticipated that over the next 20 years, the country's energy consumption would increase by 33%. The use of renewable energy may cover the gap.

Even if fossil fuels were infinitely abundant, utilizing renewable energy is better for the environment. Because they create few, if any, pollutants, renewable energy sources are often referred to as "clean" or "green." On the other hand, burning fossil fuels releases greenhouse gases into the atmosphere, trapping solar heat and causing global warming. The majority of climatologists agree that the Earth's average temperature has increased during the last century. Scientists expect that as sea levels rise, severe weather events such as floods, heat waves, droughts, and other natural disasters may become more frequent.

When fossil fuels are burnt, more pollutants are discharged into the air, land, and water. These pollutants have a severe negative impact on both individuals and the environment. Health diseases like asthma are influenced by air pollution. Fish and plants are harmed by acid rain caused by nitrogen oxides and sulfur dioxide. Additionally, nitrogen oxides contribute to smog.

We can achieve energy security and independence by using renewable energy. Since 1973, the percentage of oil that the United States imports has increased from 34% to over 50%. For instance, replacing part of our petroleum with fuels derived from plant materials might reduce costs and increase our country's energy security.

Renewable energy is widely available, and technology is constantly evolving. Renewable energy may be used in a variety of ways. In our everyday lives, the majority of us currently utilize renewable energy.

Hydropower

Our biggest and most developed renewable power source, hydropower generates around 10% of the country's electricity. There are now roughly 77,000 megawatts of hydropower available (MW). Hydroelectric power plants produce electricity by harnessing the energy of moving water. The most popular kind of hydropower employs a riverbank dam to hold back a sizable water reservoir. To produce power, water is discharged via turbines. However, "run of the river" systems redirect river water into a pipeline that leads to a turbine.

Hydropower plants don't emit any pollutants into the air, but they may have an impact on the water supply and the habitats of many animals. As a result, hydropower plants are currently being built and run in a way that has the least negative effects on rivers.

To replicate the river's natural flow, several of them are diverting a part of the flow around their dams. But even while this enhances the habitat of the river for animals, it also lowers the production of the power plant. In order to aid fish migration and reduce the amount of fish killed, other strategies including better tur- bines and fish ladders are also being deployed.

Bioenergy

The energy obtained from bio-mass (organic matter), such as plants, is known as bioenergy. You have utilized bioenergy if you have ever used a campfire or fireplace to burn wood.

However, not all of the biomass we use comes from plants or trees. Large amounts of unwanted or leftover biomass, which may be utilized as a source of bioenergy, can be produced by a variety of sectors, including those engaged in construction and the processing of agricultural goods.

Biopower

With more over 7,000 MW of installed capacity, biomass is this country's second-largest source of renewable energy after hydropower. Part utilities and power producers with coal-fired power plants have discovered that switching some of the coal with biomass is a cheap way to cut down on unwelcome emissions. Biomass might take the place of up to 15% of the coal.

Compared to coal, biomass contains less sulfur. Consequently, less sulfur dioxide is released into the atmosphere, which helps to cause acid rain. Furthermore, the use of biomass in these boilers lowers nitrous oxide emissions.

Another method of producing electricity is by a process known as gasification, which involves converting biomass into gas that is then burnt in a gas turbine. In addition to gas, mostly methane, which may be burnt in a boiler to create steam for electricity production or industrial operations, biomass decomposition in landfills also creates gas. In order to chemically transform biomass into pyrolysis oil, which is a kind of fuel oil, biomass may also be heated in the absence of oxygen. Pyrolysis oil is a feedstock for the production of fuels, chemicals, and power.

Biofuels

Direct conversion of biomass into so-called "biofuels," which are liquid fuels. Biofuels are preferred to power stationary power production and occasionally automobiles since they are portable and have a high energy density. The most popular biofuel is ethanol, an alcohol produced by fermenting biomass that contains a lot of carbs. Corn is now the main source of ethanol. To assist achieve ozone air quality regulations, several communities add ethanol to gasoline.

Additionally, there are now automobiles on the market that can run on a blend of ethanol and gasoline, such as E85, which contains 85% ethanol and 15% gasoline. Biodiesel is a different kind of biofuel that may be produced from both plant and animal fats. A car may run on biodiesel or utilize it as a fuel additive to cut pollutants.

The market for liquid fuels is dominated by biodiesel and corn ethanol to the tune of 0.4 percent. Researchers are evaluating agricultural leftovers including cornstalks and leaves, wood chips, food waste, grass, and even rubbish as viable biofuel sources in an effort to enhance the supply of biofuels that are now accessible.

Bio based Goods

Corn, wheat, soybeans, wood, and residues are examples of biomass that may be utilized to create products and chemicals that we typically get from petroleum. Cornstarch is already being used by the industry to create common plastics like shrink wrap, dining utensils, and even vehicle bumpers.

The commercial production of thermoset polymers, such as electrical switch plate covers, from leftover wood is now under research.

Solar cell types and applications

Typically, solar cells are called for the semiconducting component that makes them up. For these materials to absorb sunlight, they need to have certain properties. While some cells are tailored for usage in space, others are made to withstand sunlight that reaches the Earth's surface.

To take use of diverse absorption and charge separation techniques, solar cells may be constructed using only one layer of light-absorbing material (single-junction) or using numerous physical configurations (multi-junctions). There are three generations of solar cells: first, second, and third.

The first generation of cells, also known as conventional, traditional, or wafer-based cells, is constructed of crystalline silicon, the PV technology that is most widely used in industry and contains components like polycrystalline and monocrystalline silicon. Amorphous silicon, CdTe, and CIGS cells are among the thin-film solar cells of the second generation. These cells are economically relevant in utility-scale photovoltaic power plants, integrated photovoltaic buildings, and tiny stand-alone power systems. Several thin-film technologies, which are often referred to as emerging photovoltaic, are included in the third generation of solar cells. The majority of them is still in the research or development stages and has not yet been used commercially.

Many employ both inorganic and organic materials, frequently organometallic compounds. There is a lot of research being done on these technologies despite the fact that their efficiencies had been poor and the stability of the absorber material was often too short for practical use. This is because they promise to help produce low-cost, highly efficient solar cells. Silicon solar cells are used in "first generation" solar panels.

They are either carved from a block of silicon made up of several crystals or manufactured from a single silicon crystal (mono-crystalline) (multi-crystalline - shown at right). Thin-film solar cells of the "second generation" are less costly to make than conventional silicon solar cells since less material is needed to make them. As its name suggests, thin-film photovoltaic (PV) cells are a physically thin solar technology. They need greater surface area to produce the same amount of power, yet they are only somewhat less efficient than other varieties.

The many kinds of solar cells are as follows.

Silicon Amorphous Solar Cell (A-Si)

The non-crystalline type of silicon is called amorphous silicon (a-Si). With more than 15 years on the market, it is the thin film technology that is the most advanced. Although it is often employed in pocket calculators, it is also utilized to power a few private residences, structures, and outlying facilities. Amorphous-silicon solar cells were invented by United Solar Systems Corp. (UniSolar), which continues to be a prominent manufacturer today, along with Sharp and Sanyo.

A thin coating of silicon material, roughly 1 micrometer thick, is vapor-deposited over a substrate made of glass or metal to create amorphous silicon panels. Amorphous silicon may also be deposited on plastic since it can be done at temperatures as low as 75 degrees Celsius. The cell structure is composed of a single series of p-i-n layers in its most basic form. However, when exposed to the sun, single layer cells experience a considerable reduction in their power production (between 15% and 35%). The Staebler-Wronski Effect is the name given to the process of deterioration in honor of its discoverers. In order to boost the electric field strength across the material and provide better stability, thinner layers are necessary. This lowers light absorption, and consequently cell efficiency.

Due to this, the industry has created devices with tandem or even triple layers that include p-i-n cells layered on top of one another. Uni-

Solar is one of the innovators in the field of amorphous silicon solar cell development. They use a three layer technique that is designed to catch light from the whole solar spectrum (see figure below). The thickness of the solar cell is just 1 micron, or around 1/300th the size of a solar cell made of mono-crystalline silicon, as can be seen in the figure.

Amorphous solar cells have a yield of roughly 7% compared to crystalline silicon's output of about 18%. The Staebler-Wronski effect, which appears during the first hours that the panels are exposed to sunlight and causes a drop in energy production from 10% to roughly 7%, is partially to blame for the poor efficiency rate. Amorphous silicon solar cells' main benefit is their decreased production costs, which make them very cost-competitive.

Cellular Biohybrid Solar

A solar cell that combines organic material (photosystem I) and inorganic material is referred to as a biohybrid solar cell. Researchers from Vanderbilt University have created biohybrid solar cells. To increase the efficiency of solar energy conversion, the team mimicked the natural process of photosynthesis using the photosystem I (a photoactive protein complex found in the thylakoid membrane). This new kind of renewable energy comes from the biohybrid solar cells.

The photosystem I consists of many layers that collect photonic energy, transform it into chemical energy, and then produce a current that flows through the cell. With the exception of the injected photosystem I complexes, which are introduced and collected over many days in the gold layer, the cell itself is composed of many of the same non-organic components as those in conventional solar cells.

A thin green coating representing the photosytem I becomes apparent after a few days.

This thin coating is what facilitates and enhances the energy conversion. However, the biohybrid cell is still in the research stage.

When they began to notice and concentrate on the photosystem I protein, the Vanderbilt University team began performing research on photosynthesis. When scientists saw how extensively used and effective the protein was in converting solar energy, they began looking for ways to incorporate and advance other technology.

The scientists obtained the photosystem I from spinach. To separate the photosystem I from the thylakoid membrane, thylakoid membranes were first separated and purified.

Comparing the electrical current produced by their study to those previously produced by other solar cells, it was found to be 1000 times larger. To assist in creating the first prototype of the biohybrid solar cell, the team has been recruiting a group of student engineers. The group has also developed a second design for the photosystem II protein complex.

Inverters

By translating, filtering, and stepping voltages, inverters change DC in batteries into on- demand AC (changing them from one level to another). The output becomes cleaner as processing intensifies, but conversion efficiency suffers as a result. You'll make your decision while looking for an inverter based on the following criteria:

- The maximum sustained load. The maximum continuous watt output used to grade inverters.
- The highest surge load. An inverter will simply shut off or get damaged if you ask it to provide more power than it can. You will want an inverter with a surge capacity that is three to seven times more than the peak appliance wattage if your inverter will be required to power induction motors (such as those in your washer and dryer, dishwasher, heavy power tools, etc.). If your air conditioner uses 1,500 watts, for instance, you'll need around 5,000 watts of surge power to start the engine.

Battery voltage input (12, 24, or 48V).

- The required output voltage (120 versus 240). If 240 volts are required, a transformer must be installed or two identical inverters must be placed in series to provide 240 volts.
- The AC waveform must be pure.
- Whether you need a synchronous inverter or a static inverter. On demand, a synchronous inverter converts DC to AC and supplies it straight to the user. Any surplus power is delivered into the utility company's grid, which serves as a storage battery. You pull power from the grid when you need more of it. Inverters for the grid are another name for them.
- Add-on capabilities.

Three main waveforms are used by inverters to provide current: square wave, modified square wave (also known as modified sine wave), and pure sine wave (true sine wave). Pure sine waves are the waveform that is most similar to grid waves. Square wave inverters are cheap but only somewhat effective.

Modified square wave inverters provide improved surge capacity for starting motors as well as cost-effective power for operating gadgets and small appliances. The majority of appliances accept them.

However, certain printers, copiers, and rechargeable gadgets may be damaged or not function properly as a result. Additionally, they make fluorescent lights, fans, and audio equipment hum. Running equipment that is waveform-sensitive requires the use of pure sine wave inverters.

There are unique characteristics on certain inverters. An internal battery charger that charges batteries quickly when an AC source is attached to the inverter input terminals is an example.

The ability to move from one AC source to another or from utility power to inverter power for specific loads is another example of automatic transfer switching.

Battery temperature correction, internal relays to manage loads, and autonomous remote generator start-stop are other features that might be included. Keep in mind that there might be up to 25% efficiency losses between the source, wiring, batteries, and inverter.

Conclusion

Learning survival skills doesn't have to be a matter of life and death. Learning how to survive in the wild can be a challenging but rewarding hobby that can also boost your fitness and confidence.

Even developing a survival mindset can be a benefit in regular society, as it cultivates your self-sufficiency, problem solving and lateral thinking. However, above and beyond the everyday benefits there is a huge pragmatic and obvious reason to learn survival skills – survival.

There is no compelling reason to think that we may never be in a situation where our survival skills are truly put to test.

This doesn't mean that as a prepper you commit to conspiracy theories about the collapse of government and biochemical warfare. Perhaps you simply recognize the possibility of certain environmental hazards and take the initiative to learn to manage those situations in advance.

Alternatively, you may also realize than survival skills are important if you were to get lost.

Regardless of the reason, you have come to understand that taking the time to learning survival skills is a smart choice.

This book started you on your survival journey. By now you should know how you need to think if you want to survive difficult situations, as well as what type of disasters can occur. You know how to prepare a survival kit and how you may use its various components to collect water and find food in the wilderness.

Furthermore, you know how to build a shelter, how to start a fire and how to navigate.

This is only the beginning of learning how to survive in the wild, but it is a good foundation to build upon.

Now it is up to you to progress even further and fully master learning to how to survive in this dangerous world."